BAT MITZVAH: A JEWISH GIRL'S COMING OF AGE

I felt like I had accomplished something big in my life. Reading the Torah was a very special part. It was something I'd never done before in front of people. It was amazing to know I could do it. It's a hard thing to make music out of a bunch of words smooshed together on the page. If I had a chance to do it again, I definitely would.

Ayana Morse,
on her bat mitzvah

"With today's multiple expressions of being Jewish . . . the book should have broad appeal, as it touches on each situation."
—*School Library Journal*

"[A] relevant, informative, and highly readable companion to Kimmell's *Bar Mitzvah*." —*Booklist*

"A treasure trove of information about both Jewish women's history and contemporary bat mitzvah practices, at once engaging, accessible, and informative."
—Martha Ackelsberg, Professor of Government
and Women's Studies, Smith College

Also by Barbara Diamond Goldin:

• •

Just Enough Is Plenty: A Hanukkah Tale
Cakes and Miracles: A Purim Tale
Fire! The Beginnings of the Labor Movement
The Magician's Visit: A Passover Tale
Red Means Good Fortune: A Story of San Francisco's
Chinatown
The Passover Journey: A Seder Companion

BAT MITZVAH

A Jewish Girl's Coming of Age

by Barbara Diamond Goldin
Illustrated by Erika Weihs

PUFFIN BOOKS

PUFFIN BOOKS
Published by the Penguin Group
Penguin Putnam Inc., 375 Hudson Street, New York, New York 10014, U.S.A.
Penguin Books Ltd, 27 Wrights Lane, London W8 5TZ, England
Penguin Books Australia Ltd, Ringwood, Victoria, Australia
Penguin Books Canada Ltd, 10 Alcorn Avenue, Toronto, Ontario, Canada M4V 3B2
Penguin Books (N.Z.) Ltd, 182-190 Wairau Road, Auckland 10, New Zealand

Penguin Books Ltd, Registered Offices: Harmondsworth, Middlesex, England

First published in the United States of America by Viking,
a division of Penguin Books USA Inc., 1995
Published in Puffin Books, 1997

1 3 5 7 9 10 8 6 4 2

THE LIBRARY OF CONGRESS HAS CATALOGED THE VIKING EDITION AS FOLLOWS:
Goldin, Barbara Diamond.
Bat mitzvah : a Jewish girl's coming of age / by Barbara Diamond Goldin;
illustrated by Erika Weihs. p. cm.
Includes bibliographical references and index.
Summary: A history and description of the bat mitzvah, the ceremony in which
a Jewish girl marks her transition to adulthood.
ISBN 0-670-86034-4 (hardcover)
1. Bat mitzvah—Juvenile literature. 2. Women in Judaism—Juvenile literature. 3. Jewish
women—Religious life—Juvenile literature. [1. Bat mitzvah. 2. Women in Judaism.
3. Judaism—Customs and practices.] I. Weihs, Erika, ill. II. Title.
BM707.G64 1995 296.4'43—dc20 95-22100 CIP AC

Puffin Books ISBN 0-14-037516-3

Printed in the United States of America

The illustrations are scratchboard drawings.

For Rabbi Daniel and Hanna Tiferet Siegel, and Noah,
Shefa, and Elisha—with love

Acknowledgments

I am especially grateful to the twenty-five people I interviewed whose names appear throughout this book. In addition, I wish to thank my editor, Deborah Brodie, who had the vision for this book in the beginning and the editorial talents to help me carry out that vision.

Several people led me to sources and to thinking about the shape of this book. Thanks especially to Rabbi Sue Levi Elwell, Rabbi Philip Graubart, Hanna Tiferet Siegel, Sher Sweet, and Shoshana Zonderman. Emily Milner helped me find appropriate articles at the Jewish Women's Resource Center in New York City; Joseph C. and Sharon Penkower Kaplan led me to some of my interviewees; and the members of my writing group gave me support and valuable criticism.

Several experts read the manuscript-in-progress and shared their much welcomed expertise with us: Martha Ackelsberg, Professor of Government and Women's Studies at Smith College; Judith Herschlag Muffs, Judaica consultant; Rabbi Aaron Panken of Congregation Rodeph Sholom, New York City; and Judith Plaskow, Professor of Religious Studies, Manhattan College. Many thanks.

For their contributions to the jacket montage, we are very grateful to Carey Ascenzo; Ilana Blatt-Eisengart; Gavriela M. Bogin-Farber; Thalia Brown; Kim Hayes; Anne Golomb Hoffman; Leon Hoffman, M.D.; Liora Hoffman; Sarah Horowitz; Danielle Johannessen; Kate Lefko-Everett; J. Levine Books and Judaica, New York City; Nina Morris-Farber; Alison Rodin; Joyce Slochower; Rochelle Sparko; Sharon and Rabbi Michael Strassfeld; Betsy Platkin Teutsch; Leora Visotzky; and the staff of Congregation Ansche Chesed, New York City. And especially to Stephanie Garcia for her creative expertise and flair in putting it all together.

B.D.G.

CONTENTS

Preface xi
Introduction 1

Part One: The Women's Story

The First Bat Mitzvah 5
Matriarchs and Prophets, Warriors and Judges: The Jewish
Woman in Biblical Times 10
Divorce Decrees, Tax Registers, and the Talmud: The Jewish
Woman in Talmudic Times and Late Antiquity 19
Arranged Marriages and Secret Jews: The Jewish Woman
in the Middle Ages 22
Hearing from Women Themselves: The Jewish Woman in
the 1500s and 1600s 30
"It Was the Beginning of Things": The Jewish Woman from
the 1700s to Modern Times 35

Part Two: Ceremony and Celebration

Don't Forget to Study: Preparation 51
What's Going On Up There?: The Ceremony 83
"What Chocolate-Covered Strawberries?": Celebrating 110
Is It Really All Over?: Afterward 118
Glossary 124
Notes on Sources 132
Index 135

PREFACE

When I was thirteen, in 1959, the girls in my Conservative synagogue in Philadelphia did not have the same coming-of-age ceremony that the boys had.

I was told that I could have "something" on Friday night. But I didn't want "something." I wanted the real thing—to read out of the Torah, the Five Books of Moses, to chant the haftarah, the reading from the Prophets, and to lead services on Saturday morning. So I chose not to do anything to mark my coming of age in Judaism.

I have two younger brothers; each became a bar mitzvah in our synagogue. They learned to chant the service, as well as Torah and haftarah, and regularly led junior congregation services on Saturday mornings. I went often too and sang, but I could never lead. That was only for the boys.

Yet I was the one who continued Hebrew school until I was seventeen, while my brothers had stopped by fifteen. I was a bit confused. Here I was allowed to go to Religious School, but not allowed to participate fully in the Jewish life which I loved.

I don't think I actually said all this to my parents or to anyone else. I'm not even sure I knew how angry and disappointed I was at the time. Many of these feelings were unexpressed and came out only later, little by little.

Something else added to my conflicted feelings over what I was taught and what I could do as a girl within Judaism as I knew it: the stories about my grandma Rose.

Rose had some Jewish education in Eastern Europe before she immigrated to America. Unlike many of her contemporaries, she could even read Hebrew.

When the holidays came, the other women would want to know where Grandma Rose was going to sit. (In an Orthodox synagogue, the women sit in a separate section, often behind a curtain or in the balcony.) By sitting near her, they could hear her chant the Hebrew in the prayer book, which they couldn't read. In this way, they could follow the service.

In the 1930s, Grandma Rose convinced the rabbi and the other men in his Saturday afternoon study group to let her study Torah with them. My mother would tell me, "Your grandma Rose said she knew as much as the men, so why couldn't she study Torah, too?"

Grandma Rose also felt strongly that women had a right to an education and a right to work outside the home. Yet Grandma Rose was an observant Orthodox Jew. She kept a kosher home, celebrated all the holidays, and didn't complain about sitting in the women's section at the synagogue.

With all the stories about Grandma Rose floating around, my parents shouldn't have been too surprised by my negative reaction to a token ceremony when I was thirteen.

Twenty years later, in the late 1970s, I finally found a *minyan,* a prayer group, that allowed women to do the same things as men in a service. The leaders of this *minyan,* Rabbi Daniel Siegel and Hanna Tiferet Siegel, went even further. They encouraged women to add their own innovations.

I experienced many firsts in this *minyan*, but the first time I held the Torah stands out especially in my mind. We were standing in a circle when the rabbi took the Torah scroll out of the Ark. It was passed around so each of us could hold it for a short time and then pass it on. After all those years of seeing the Torah from far away, I was very moved to be able to touch it and hold it close.

In the late 1980s, I read out of the Torah scroll for the first time. And at my daughter Josee's bat mitzvah ceremony in 1992, I read a longer section of the Torah. I felt a real sense of participation in her ceremony.

Since then I have been studying to become a bar and bat mitzvah tutor and have chanted three *haftarot* before my congregation. I felt very nervous before chanting the haftarah, and proud and relieved afterward. Now I understand a little of how a twelve- or thirteen-year-old girl or boy must feel preparing for and being the major participant, the star, of her or his ceremony.

Today, when I see a bat mitzvah ceremony, I think about how lucky this girl is. She does not know of a time when a twelve- or thirteen-year-old girl would not have been able to do all that she does on this day.

And that is why I wrote this book. I'm glad a girl today can become a bat mitzvah in a public ceremony and not be excluded from a role of leadership in the synagogue. But I also want girls to know of the struggles of all the women through the centuries who made this possible.

This book is for all those girls who are looking forward to their coming-of-age ceremony. It is also for their friends who are being invited to this ceremony and don't have a clue about what's going on, and for the parents and teachers of both.

In the first section, you will read about some of the women in Jewish history whose stories have come down to us. This section could have been a whole book in itself—there are so many more women we are learning about as we uncover women's history. The development of the bat mitzvah ceremony is part of this work of reexamining and recovering the role of women in Judaism—in history, in ritual, and today.

In the second section, you will find out how girls prepare for their ceremony, what happens at the ceremony (or, "What's going on up there?"), and what happens afterward. I have interviewed girls and women from all over the United States, and you'll be able to read what they have to say about becoming a bat mitzvah.

You'll see that there are many variations in the whole process. However, a few things seem to be almost always the same—the girls—or women—are nervous beforehand and filled with pride afterward. They've worked hard, enjoyed being the center of attention, and felt it was a very important day in their lives, well worth all the work. Some, though not all, felt it was an experience that transformed them.

If you are reading this book because you are getting ready for your own bat mitzvah ceremony, I wish you this: May your day be very special and meaningful. May you remember all the women in our past, in our tradition, who lived in different times, eras of different possibilities. May you have a vision too, as they did, and work just as hard to realize it.

And above all—don't forget to study!

INTRODUCTION

Bar or *bat mitzvah* is the Hebrew phrase for the coming of age. One becomes responsible for one's own actions and for fulfilling religious obligations. Becoming a bar or bat mitzvah does not have to be marked formally in a synagogue or home by a ceremony or party. When Jewish girls reach twelve or Jewish boys thirteen years of age, they become responsible for carrying out the religious duties of a Jewish adult, taking themselves and Judaism seriously.

This idea was expressed by a second-century C.E. scholar, Rabbi Judah ben Tema, who said that at thirteen a child is ready to carry out the commandments. Because most girls begin to mature physically at an earlier age than boys, twelve, not thirteen, was the age chosen for a girl's passage to adulthood.

By the thirteenth century, references to the bar mitzvah indicate that it was an accepted custom to recognize a boy at thirteen in some way, such as by having the rabbi bless him. By the sixteenth century in Europe, the form of the ceremony for boys had become more like today's.

On the Sabbath, the day of rest, coinciding with or immediately after his thirteenth birthday, the boy was called up to the Torah scroll, which contains the Five Books of Moses handwritten on parchment by a religious scribe, to say the blessings and to read from it. Often a festive meal was held in his home afterward and the boy gave a talk dealing with some aspect of the bar mitzvah ceremony.

We do not read of celebrations for a Jewish girl's coming of age until about the 1800s, in countries such as France, Italy, and Germany, when there is evidence that families would sometimes have a special meal in their home for their daughter's twelfth birthday. The girl might deliver a talk at that time. However it wasn't until the mid-1900s that girls could participate in a ceremony similar to the boys' at this important time in their lives.

In many synagogues today, girls and boys are trained for their ceremonies in the same way. In other Jewish communities, the bat mitzvah ceremony may be different from a boy's, and in some there is no ceremony at all.

The first section of this book will give you an idea of the history of Jewish women—the history behind the bat mitzvah ceremony today. In the second section, you can read about the actual ceremony in all its variations.

PART ONE

··

THE WOMEN'S STORY

THE FIRST BAT MITZVAH

A sunny Saturday in early May of 1922 marked a major event in the history of Jewish women: the first bat mitzvah ceremony in North America.

Judith Kaplan had mixed feelings about the upcoming ceremony. She liked all the attention she was getting, yet she was worried about what her friends would say. Would they tease her for being different? Although some of them had learned to speak Hebrew, as Judith had, none of them had had a special ceremony in a synagogue to celebrate their becoming a bat mitzvah. Actually, until a few months before, there had been no synagogue that would even allow such a celebration.

Most of all, Judith was worried because as of Friday her father, Rabbi Mordecai Kaplan (who was to become the founder of a branch of Judaism called Reconstructionist Judaism), had not yet decided what Judith's part in the ceremony would be. And the ceremony was the very next day, the Sabbath, the Jewish day of rest that begins at sundown on Friday and lasts until nightfall on Saturday.

Finally, after the Friday night meal, her father called Judith into his study, where she practiced the blessings she would say before and after the Torah readings, the readings from the Five Books of Moses in the Bible. She also practiced reading a section of the weekly Torah portion in both Hebrew and English.

At the synagogue the next morning, she sat with the men in the room that held the *bimah,* the platform from which the Torah is read. Her mother, younger sisters, and disapproving grandmothers all sat in the separate section for the women, as was traditional.

Judith's father was the one who read from the Torah scroll and chanted the haftarah, the weekly portion from the Prophets. Not until the Torah scroll was covered did Judith chant the first blessing, read the selection her father had chosen for her (from her own Bible), and finish with the closing blessing.

Unlike many of today's girls, Judith did not chant from the actual Torah scroll, or even stand near it. She sat below the *bimah* at a "respectable distance" from the holy scroll.

Still, Judith's ceremony was a first, the first time a girl was presented in a synagogue as a bat mitzvah. And, as she says herself, "No thunder sounded, no lightning struck. The institution of bat mitzvah had been born without incident, and the rest of the day was all rejoicing."

During the decades that followed, other synagogues began to accept the public ceremony of bat mitzvah. And during these decades,

Jewish women all over North America fought for changes that would allow them to participate more fully in community religious life.

This struggle by Jewish women, and men like Rabbi Kaplan, for equality in the synagogue, was occurring at the same time that women in the nation as a whole were fighting for their rights as citizens. In 1920, for instance, the Nineteenth Amendment to the United States Constitution was passed, giving women the right to vote.

Women's struggle for the vote in the United States had been going on since the 1840s, when women joined the antislavery movement and learned to speak in public and to petition their congressmen.

One woman, Elizabeth Cady Stanton, went to England with her husband as a delegate to an antislavery convention in 1840. To her horror, she found that not only were women delegates not allowed to speak at this convention, they had to sit behind curtains and could not watch what went on. (Jewish women weren't the only ones behind a curtain!)

There she met another American delegate, Lucretia Mott, who was equally enraged. The two decided to hold a convention in the United States after their return to demand rights for women, including the right to vote. This convention took place in 1848.

These women and others like Susan B. Anthony worked hard. In 1860, they had succeeded in getting the New York Assembly to pass the Married Women's Property Act, giving a married woman control over her own property and earnings. Before this act, the husband controlled them.

Getting the vote took longer. An amendment giving women the vote was turned down by Congress in 1878. It wasn't until the 1920s, a

7

time of great prosperity and great change in general, that women finally won the right to vote.

The twenties were a liberating decade for women. Electricity became more readily available in homes, which made electrical appliances, such as vacuum cleaners and washing machines, possible. Women did not have to spend hours cleaning, or an entire day every week doing family laundry anymore.

The rise of the flappers made front-page news. These were women who cut their hair short, raised the hemlines of their skirts, and behaved in unconventional ways in public.

More and more unmarried women had paying jobs. Besides being factory workers, teachers, nurses, telephone and typewriter operators, they also became reporters, college professors, musicians, and editors.

This was the atmosphere surrounding Judith Kaplan at the time of the first bat mitzvah ceremony. In the years since then, we have seen many changes in the roles of women in both American life and Jewish life. In 1949, Judith's father's congregation became the first to count women in the religious quorum called a *minyan*. The congregation also became the first to allow women to be called up to the Torah scroll to chant the blessings. In 1972, Sally Priesand was ordained at Hebrew Union College-Jewish Institute of Religion in Cincinnati— the first woman rabbi.

Today's young women and men may not even realize that there was a time when no synagogue would sponsor a bat mitzvah ceremony. Rabbi Sue Levi Elwell, founding director of the American Jewish Congress Feminist Center in Los Angeles, tells a story about an educational director of a large synagogue who was speaking to a group of her students. When the director told them she had never had a bat mitzvah ceremony, one student said, "Why? Did you convert to Judaism?" Another asked, "Did you come here from Russia?" They were all surprised when she answered simply, "No, I was a girl. And when I was young, girls did not have a bat mitzvah ceremony."

Why haven't girls had the same ceremony as their male counterparts throughout Jewish history? Why is the bat mitzvah ceremony such a recent phenomenon? And why is it still not accepted by all Jews?

The answer lies in the way Jewish girls and women have been viewed in Judaism—and how women have been viewed in society as a whole. Women's lives were expected to be focused on the home much more than men's were.

Traditionally, the Jewish woman's role was to prepare for the holidays, light the holiday and Sabbath candles, keep a kosher home, bake the holiday and Sabbath breads, use the ritual bath called the *mikvah* at prescribed times, and take care of her husband and children. Women were exempt from particular commandments that the men were required to follow, such as praying three times a day and studying Torah, which would take time away from home duties.

However, as we look through Jewish history, we find exceptions to this picture of Jewish women. Women now are reexamining and recovering their history. In the process, they are discovering more and more women who can serve as good role models for today, even though they may have lived long ago in Biblical or Talmudic times, or in the Middle Ages.

MATRIARCHS AND PROPHETS, WARRIORS AND JUDGES

··
The Jewish Woman in Biblical Times

In the Bible, we read of women who were Matriarchs and prophets, judges, shepherds, and warriors, as well as wives, mothers, sisters, and daughters. The stories in the Bible are rich and varied, not about women who did only as they were told. These women's lives and personalities were as complicated as those of people today.

In the beginning there was Eve, the first woman, made from Adam's rib, who ate from the forbidden fruit of the Tree of Knowledge. What choice would you have made if you were in Eve's bare feet? Knowledge or eternal life in the Garden of Eden?

Then there were the four Matriarchs. Sarah, wife of Abraham, was the first. She laughed when an angel told her that she would bear a son in her old age—she who had not been able to conceive in all those years. When her son was born, she named him Isaac, which means *laughter* in Hebrew.

So many of the women of the Bible had trouble conceiving children. And if they could bear children, the emphasis was on producing sons, not daughters. In those days, a woman might have to give her husband a handmaid who could bear his child, as Sarah had done. Or, since this was a time when all men could take more than one wife (as is still true in some parts of the world today), they would have to stand by and see his other wives bear his children. We can see the foremothers' anguish and their difficult choices right there in the ancient text.

After Isaac's birth Sarah faced a dilemma: What should she do about her Egyptian handmaid Hagar and Hagar's son, Ishmael? Ishmael was older than her Isaac. He teased and mocked Isaac, saying, "It doesn't matter what you do. I am the firstborn."

Sarah asked Abraham to send Hagar and Ishmael away. Though reluctant, Abraham did so, knowing that God had said Isaac, not Ishmael, was to be his heir.

What would you have done in Sarah's place? After all, this was a time when being a firstborn son, receiving your father's blessing, and being heir to his property meant everything.

The second Matriarch, Rebekah, showed her helpfulness and kindness to strangers at the local well. She watered the camels belonging to Abraham's servant, Eliezer, without being asked, and thus was chosen to be Isaac's wife. She bore the twins Esau and Jacob, Esau being the older.

Rebekah was faced with the problem of knowing which son would be the better leader of his people. While she was pregnant with the twins, she had been told by God, "Two nations are in your womb. . . . And the elder shall serve the younger." She struggled to make this

11

come about, in a time when women's power could only be undercover, behind the scenes, and depended more on cunning than anything else. Rebekah chose to tell Jacob how to deceive his father—with the hairy arm trick (Genesis, 27:1–46)—and so win the blessing meant for his brother.

Rachel and Leah, the third and fourth Matriarchs, were sisters who both married Jacob. Just as Jacob had deceived his father, he was deceived in turn. He worked seven years for Rachel and Leah's father, in order to earn his bride. He had been promised Rachel, but with the morning light, he found that the veiled woman he had been married to was Leah, the older sister. Yet it was still Rachel whom he loved.

He did marry Rachel a week later, and had to work another seven years for her. This made a total of fourteen years that Jacob worked for his father-in-law, Laban, in order to pay both sisters' bride price. (Jacob surely could have used his mother's help on this deal!)

Imagine being one of the sisters married to the same man. Imagine that it is your sister who is the beautiful one and better loved by your husband. You, Leah, were not even chosen by him. He was deceived into marrying you. Complicate this story with the fact that you can bear children easily, while your sister Rachel cannot and succeeds only after many years of trying.

The feelings of these women are not always clearly stated in the Bible, but we can sense them by reading between the lines. We can feel the jealousy and love, sadness, joy and anguish, strength, courage and longing, anger and kindness of all four of the Matriarchs.

Think of these four women as you stand on the *bimah* reading from the Torah, or listen to it being read—these women who lived thousands of years ago and whose lives still speak to us today. They were strong women who made choices and took risks, who did not stand by meekly.

After the Matriarchs, we learn in the Bible of other women— including the prophet Miriam who played such an important role in the story of the Israelites' Exodus from Egypt and their wanderings in the desert.

Miriam helped her brother Moses to safety when he was a baby who had been left in a basket on the Nile. When all Israelite boy babies were supposed to be drowned by order of Pharaoh, Miriam and her mother devised a plan that allowed Moses to survive.

How do you think Miriam felt as she crouched hidden in the reeds by the Nile River, watching her baby brother's basket float quietly by her? What thoughts went through her mind? And how much courage must it have taken for her to show herself when Pharaoh's daughter came to look into the basket. Would you have been able to step forward and ask, "Princess, would you like me to find a woman to nurse this baby?"

Miriam continued to play an important role in Jewish history. For example, an old Jewish tradition tells that when the Israelites left Egypt, they left in two groups, one led by Miriam, and the other group by her younger brother Moses.

And there is a legend that when the Israelites were wandering in the desert after the liberation from Egypt, a well of fresh water accompanied them. It was called Miriam's Well, because the life-giving water was linked to Miriam's presence and her merit. She was a source of sustenance for her people.

The Book of Numbers tells us of the daughters of a man of Miriam's time named Zelophehad, who had no sons to inherit his

property when he died. During this time, only sons could be heirs. Zelophehad's five daughters went before Moses and all the people and asked that they be made the heirs. Because of their plea, a new law was created in Israel. If a man died without leaving a son, his property would be transferred to his daughter. This was quite an innovative law for that time, over three thousand years ago.

Much later, after the Israelites had settled in the Promised Land of Canaan, other women became leaders. The Book of Judges tells about Deborah, a judge, prophet, military advisor, and poet who lived at a time when the land was still divided among the different tribes of Israel.

Deborah convinced General Barak to lead an army of ten thousand men in battle against the Canaanites—no easy task, since the Canaanites had nine hundred iron chariots! Barak, whose faith was not as great as Deborah's, answered, "If you will go with me, I will go; if not, I will not go."

Deborah went with Barak, and the Israelites were victorious in that battle on Mount Tabor. Deborah was able to return to judge her people in peace. Under her influence, the land was tranquil for forty years.

Another story about Deborah shows her prophetic vision. Before the battle on Mount Tabor, she told Barak that he would not be the one to kill Sisera, the Canaanite army commander. Instead, God would deliver Sisera into the hands of a woman. And it *was* a woman, Yael, who invited the fleeing Sisera into her tent, fed him, and then killed him by driving a tent peg through his forehead while he slept. Picture inviting the leader of the enemy army into your tent, and then doing him in without having taken martial arts lessons!

You wouldn't say the Biblical Ruth was heroic, not in the same way as Yael or Deborah. But Ruth was loyal. When her mother-in-law, Naomi, returned to the Promised Land after her husband and sons died, Ruth went with her. The famous lines "Wherever you go, I will go; wherever you lodge, I will lodge; your people shall be my people, and your God my God" were Ruth's. This Moabite woman, a convert to Judaism, married a kinsman of Naomi's named Boaz and became the great-grandmother of a future king of Israel, David. Would you have made the choice Ruth did? To go to a strange land and live among a strange people? This was courage, too.

Another famous woman of the Bible, in the Book of Samuel, was Hannah, who like Sarah and Rachel, could not bear a child. Hannah was well loved by her husband, Elkanah. But Elkanah's other wife, Peninah, had children and taunted Hannah mercilessly. Finally, Hannah went to the Temple to pray for a child. She prayed so fervently that the priest Eli believed she was drunk, until Hannah explained her distress.

God heard Hannah, and her prayers were answered. A son, Samuel, was born to her. As she had promised, Hannah brought him into the service of God in the care of the priest Eli. Samuel later became the famous prophet who anointed Saul and David, the first and second kings of Israel.

After Hannah, we come to another Biblical woman, Michal, daughter of King Saul and wife of David, Ruth's great-grandson. Michal's story would make a great, action-packed movie—in fact, it has.

Over time the relationship between her father, King Saul, and her husband, David, became more and more difficult and dangerous. Saul knew that David was the favorite of the people and the old prophet Samuel, Hannah's son. He knew his very throne was in jeopardy.

So one night, Saul sent soldiers to surround the home of David and Michal, with the intention of killing David. Putting her own life in danger, Michal lowered David out a window. She then stuffed his bed, so it looked like there was a person under the covers.

Try to picture yourself as Michal, standing by your husband David's bed, waiting for your father's soldiers to storm your house. You are trying to decide what you will say to them, and to your father.

Later, in the book of the Bible called Esther, we learn about a Jew who became queen of Persia. At her cousin Mordecai's suggestion, Esther kept her religion a secret from her husband the king and the other members of court. She could serve her people best by being cautious in this time of persecution. Think about how hard a secret that would be to keep and the intrigue involved when your religion affected every aspect of your life, even the food you ate. (It is said that Esther had to eat a lot of chickpeas while she lived in the palace because the meat would not have been prepared according to Jewish dietary laws.)

But the most difficult time for Esther came when Mordecai told her of the prime minister Haman's wicked plot to kill all the Jews of the land. Mordecai told Esther that she was the only one in a position to save her people. Would you have risked your life, as Esther did, to save your people?

Though we long for more detail and stories about the actual daily lives of the women of those times, we do learn from the Bible, as you can see, that women played important roles in Jewish history. And we can imagine their feelings when they made their decisions and changed the lives of all who came after them. We can imagine the uncertainty of taking the first bite; their persistence and determination to see a particular son become the inheritor; their bravery in war and in situations of intense persecution; their belief in turning to prayer and God in times of anguish and victory.

Reading and knowing about these women of the Bible connects us to them and helps us reclaim women's history, a process important to a girl becoming a bat mitzvah, becoming a Jewish woman.

DIVORCE DECREES, TAX REGISTERS, AND THE TALMUD

···
The Jewish Woman in Talmudic Times and Late Antiquity

For the women who came later, we still have to imagine how they felt, what they knew and thought about. The men who recorded the history of Talmudic times and late antiquity wrote little about women's lives. And we have few sources from women for any time before the modern period.

Some information about the women who lived after Biblical times and before the Middle Ages is available. The sources include inscriptions on tombs, papyruses containing legal transactions such as divorce decrees and tax registers, and the Talmud.

The Talmud, also called the Oral Torah, was the product of the first five centuries of the Common Era. It contains stories, legal discussions, and explanations by the Rabbis on how to apply Biblical laws to their own time.

One of the women the Talmud tells us about is Queen Salome, the last independent ruler of Judea. It is said that because she was so pious, Israel prospered during her reign—even the grain crops grew to extraordinary size.

However, there were many opposing factions within Israel at the time, and Salome had to do an amazing juggling act to keep peace in the land. She had an especially tough time with her husband, Alexander Yannai, who deliberately made fun of religious traditions. Once, the people became angry with him and pelted him with *etrogim,* an Israeli citrus fruit (the Biblical equivalent of rotten eggs and tomatoes!).

In the Talmud, we also find the story of Rachel, daughter of Kalba Savua, one of the richest men in Jerusalem during the first and second centuries C.E. Rachel fell in love with Akiva, a poor, illiterate shepherd. She bravely insisted on marrying him despite her father's disapproval and threat to disown her. She never regretted her decision, though they lived in such poverty that they had only straw to sleep on. She believed so in Akiva that through her insistance, encouragement, and sacrifice, he became one of the greatest rabbi-scholars of all time.

There was the brilliant scholar and teacher Bruriah, a woman of the first and second centuries C.E., whose opinions on Jewish law are quoted in the Talmud. One story tells us that when their two sons died suddenly, Bruriah broke the news to her husband, Rabbi Meir, by asking him a question:

"If a friend gave me some jewels for safekeeping and now wants them back, should I return them?"

Her husband answered, "Of course."

Bruriah then showed Rabbi Meir their two precious sons. "Now we must return the jewels that God has entrusted to us," she said.

Archaeological sources also tell us a little about Jewish women of this time. For instance, donation and burial inscriptions show that women owned property and slaves and were sometimes the heads of households. These inscriptions often name women, for example, Rufina of Smyrna (Asia Minor), of the third century B.C.E. For once, we are not left with namelessness and anonymity for the women of 2000 years ago.

Some women, such as Sophia of Gortyn on Crete and Theopempte of Myndos in Asia Minor, were recorded as heads of synagogues and members of councils of elders in Crete, North Africa, and Italy in the fourth and fifth centuries C.E. Other women are listed and named as giving financial contributions to and attending synagogues.

So, on the one hand, we know that most Jewish women's lives (and the lives of women in the surrounding cultures) in these times were spent in their homes, caring for their households, spinning and weaving, grinding corn and baking bread, and nursing children. But we also know that some of these women were publicly active in their communities as well.

ARRANGED MARRIAGES
AND SECRET JEWS
The Jewish Woman in the Middle Ages

During the next period of history, the Middle Ages, from roughly 600 C.E. to the 1500s, Jews lived in countries all over the world. They followed Jewish laws, yet were influenced by the ways of the people around them. There were more Jews living in the Muslim countries that now make up Iraq, Egypt, North Africa, and Spain than in Europe at this time. Jewish communities flourished under the relatively tolerant Muslim rule.

Conditions in Europe, however, were becoming more restrictive as Europe became more Christian. In the middle of the fifteenth century, in some places, Jews were required to wear badges and other kinds of distinctive clothing. They were often forced to live in restricted areas called ghettos, and they were expelled from some countries altogether. Jews were permitted to enter only a few professions, such as peddling, international trade, and moneylending, the latter because Christians viewed it as a sin to lend other Christians money and charge interest.

Once again, through most of the period, we have no writings by women that reflect or tell us of Jewish women's personal lives and inner struggles. What we do have are written decisions by rabbis concerning women and legal records such as marriage contracts.

Some evidence of women's lives has also come to us from an old *genizah* discovered in a Cairo synagogue. A *genizah* is a storage place for sacred documents that are no longer being used. The documents cannot be destroyed, because they contain God's name, and so they are stored or buried. Sometimes discarded secular writings are kept in a *genizah* as well.

The papers found in the Cairo *genizah,* the marriage contracts, personal letters, and responses of local rabbis to questions, tell us about Jewish life in Egypt and the surrounding countries from the ninth to the thirteenth centuries. We know that, in general, women of this era continued to be offered much less education than men, and their lives continued to be home-based. Yet there are records, here and in other places, of women who managed their own finances, operated schools, were midwives and doctors, textile merchants, brokers, and scribes.

We do know about some things that strongly affected women's lives during this era. In Western Europe, it was the custom for Jewish girls to be married young, at eleven or twelve, to someone almost their age, while their sisters in the Jewish-Islamic world were often married at thirteen or fourteen to an older man. In these times, marriages were still arranged by the parents of the bride- and bridegroom-to-be. (Aren't you glad some things have changed?)

We also know that one of the few ways a woman could keep some financial security of her own was through her dowry. If they could afford it, the parents of the bride-to-be gave their daughter money and possessions on the occasion of her marriage. The possessions would include such items as jewelry, clothing, bedding, carpets, and other household goods. The kind of dowry a girl's parents could provide determined what kind of match would be made for her.

Women retained the rights to the value of their dowries in the cases of divorce or the death of their husbands. This is why a widow could often be more independent than a married or never-married woman. The dowry also existed in Islamic and Christian communities, where it sometimes took a slightly different form. In Islam, for example, it was the *groom* who gave the bride a dowry as protection in case of widowhood or divorce.

During this period of history a rabbi in Europe ruled that men could no longer marry more than one woman at a time. It was Rabbi Gershom ben Judah (960–1028) who forbade polygyny, the practice of having more than one wife at a time, among Eastern European Jews. He also stated that no woman could be divorced against her will. Actually, polygyny was already somewhat rare in Western Europe by this time, but neither rare nor forbidden in Muslim countries.

Despite the limitations placed on Jewish women of the Middle Ages by both Jewish tradition and the customs or laws of the societies in which they lived, there were still women who managed to have an outstanding impact on their communities.

For instance, in the 1100s, Namnah of Baghdad was so well versed in Talmud that she taught male students. They listened to her talks from outside her window where they could hear her but not see her. In this way, they did not break any of the rules of modesty pertaining to men's and women's interactions.

Another woman in the Muslim world who had a great impact on her community was Boula Ashkenazi, a doctor in Turkey in the 1500s who cured Sultan Ahmed I of smallpox. Later on she was able to intercede with him on behalf of her Jewish people to save them from being exiled from Turkey.

We know even more about Benvenida Abrabanel (1490–1560) who was from a famous Spanish-Portuguese, or Sephardic, Jewish family.

She lived during the time of the Spanish Inquisition, when the Catholic Church set up courts and judges throughout Spain, Portugal, and their colonies to discover, interrogate, and kill heretics and to probe the people's beliefs in the church's doctrine. Jews were either forced to convert to Catholicism or expelled. A convert who was suspected of "Judaizing"—continuing to carry out Jewish practices—would be tortured and often killed. At that time, Marrano was a derogatory term for the new Christian, as was *converso*.

Benvenida's uncle, Don Isaac Abrabanel, was the greatest rabbinic authority of his time and also financier to Queen Isabella. When the queen expelled all the Jews from Spain in 1492, she told Rabbi Isaac that he could stay. But he chose to stand solidly by his people and leave with them.

In exile in Italy, Benvenida ran the family banking business after the death of her husband, Samuel, in 1517. She is reported to have provided the funds to ransom more than a thousand Jewish captives. She also used her influence with the Duchess of Tuscany to negotiate a postponement of a decree that would have expelled the Jews of Southern Italy in 1541.

Also of Spanish-Portuguese origin was Doña Gracia Nasi (1510–

69) who was born into a Portuguese *converso* family of which many members were actually crypto-Jews—people who secretly practiced Judaism.

Her husband's wealth was in banking, gems, and spices. After his death, Doña Gracia left Portugal for Antwerp with her family and headed a bank there.

Once out of Portugal, Doña Gracia set up a fund to try to halt the activities of the Inquisition in Spain and Portugal. She also established a secret organization to get Jews out of these countries. This organization was much like the Underground Railroad in the United States in pre–Civil War days. Her business agents in different cities provided the secret stations that helped Jews flee the Inquisition.

Doña Gracia found herself fleeing from one Italian city-state to another, as each became unsafe for her as a crypto-Jew. She eventually moved to Constantinople, Turkey, at the invitation of the sultan. There she built a business of wool, spice, shipbuilding, shipping, and international banking. She also continued her activities on behalf of persecuted Jews the world over.

For instance, when she learned that Pope Paul IV had imprisoned one hundred *conversos* from Ancona, Italy, and had already burned twenty-five of them at the stake, she used her influence with the sultan to have him seize and take into custody all ships from Ancona that were docked in Turkish ports. She also persuaded the sultan to write the pope urging him to release the remaining *conversos*. Lastly, she organized a boycott of the Ancona port by Jewish merchants. Although not totally successful, hers was the first attempt in history by a Jew to use international economic pressure against persons who were persecuting Jews.

Doña Gracia also worked for the establishment of a safe haven for Jews in the land of Israel. Through an arrangement with the sultan, the city of Tiberias and seven surrounding villages in Israel were rebuilt as places where Jews could live. Houses, schools, and even a silk manufacturing business were built there. Doña Gracia died, however, before she could move to, or even visit, Tiberias.

Both Benvenida Abrabanel and Doña Gracia were widows—and so, as noted earlier, could hold more independent and influential positions than most women. They had an enormous impact on the societies in which they lived, and serve as good models for what women could do, even in the Middle Ages. Think of them as you study Jewish or world history in school. Where are these women and all the others on the pages of your textbook? Jewish women's history *is* there, waiting to be discovered, uncovered, and shared.

Other fascinating stories about powerful Jewish women of the Middle Ages, in both Muslim and Christian countries, tell of the dangers that accompanied political intrigue in high places.

We know of Polcelina, the mistress of the French count Theobald of Blois in the 1100s, who became involved in political intrigues at his court which grew out of the jealousy of others over the count's fondness for her. As a result, the Jews of Blois were accused of murdering a Christian boy, though his body was never found. Because of pressure from the church, the count ordered more than thirty Jews burned. Among them, and at her own wish, was Polcelina.

Another Jewish woman with an interesting history is Licoricia of Winchester in the 1200s. A successful businesswoman who had dealings with the king of England and his court, she was twice thrown into prison on charges that were later dismissed. She made large donations to the building of the famous Westminster Abbey, but like Polcelina, met a violent end, being murdered in 1277.

Perhaps the most intriguing story of a Jewish woman with behind-the-scenes political power belongs to Esther Kiera of Constantinople in the late 1500s, just a little after Doña Gracia's time. Esther and her husband started out as peddlers selling cosmetics and jewelry to the women of the sultan's harem. After her husband's death, Esther concentrated more and more on providing services to the women of the harem and became their link with the outside world.

The women of the harem were very restricted. They could have no contact with any men outside their families. The only men allowed into the harem were the sultan and his eunuchs. These women often needed the services of a woman who could move about more freely than they could. So Esther carried messages, obtained cosmetics, and assisted in childbirths. In all, she served the harems of three sultans, and was a close friend of at least one sultana.

In return for her services, Esther received various privileges from the sultan. Her influence in court affairs is shown by the fact that she was hired by the Christian city-state of Venice and by such famous people as Catherine de Médicis to act as a go-between with the sultan and his court. She was also able to help some individuals obtain titles and positions in the military and in the administration.

Through all this, Esther Kiera did not forget her Jewish people. She supported rabbis and scholars, fed the poor, financed the publication of scholarly works, and intervened on behalf of Jewish merchants when they had difficulties with the government.

Like the Biblical Esther, who saved her people from total destruction in ancient Persia, this later Esther helped to reverse a decree of Sultan Murad III that would have annihilated the Jewish communities of the Ottoman Empire.

However, unlike the Biblical Esther, but like Polcelina and Licoricia before her, Esther's life ended violently. A mob broke into the harem in 1600 to seize her, partly because of an unpopular military appointment which she had secured, and partly in an effort to undermine the power of the sultana.

Esther Kiera's story is so exotic and interesting that she appeared as a character in several European novels after her death.

HEARING FROM WOMEN THEMSELVES

The Jewish Woman in the 1500s and 1600s

By the 1500s, the end of the Middle Ages, we begin to see a change in the Jewish woman's story. We begin to hear from women themselves, in their poetry, prayers, and learned works. Women are less and less the "Anonymous" on books and paintings, and in history. More and more they have a voice, a name, and stories we can discover and learn from.

One such woman is Sarra Coppio Sullam (1592–1641). She was born into a well-known Italian Jewish family in Venice, and received a good education, both Jewish and classical. She was an accomplished writer and poet who hosted a salon. Her home became a gathering place for writers and artists, many of whom were Christian. Because of her position in the cultural life of Venice, acquaintances and friends often tried to convince her to convert to Christianity.

She wrote a pamphlet, which has been passed down to us, in which she courageously answers and refutes the accusation of a priest,

Baldassar Bonifaccio, in 1621. He accused her of denying the immortality of the soul, a charge that could have had serious consequences for Sarra in Catholic Venice.

Despite the example of Sarra Coppio Sullam, the average Jewish woman of this period was not well educated, as is true of women in general at this time (as well as many men!). Jewish women often could not read Hebrew and so could not read prayer books. (Most Jewish men were taught to read Hebrew in special religious schools.)

However, many of the Jewish women of Eastern Europe could read in their daily language, Yiddish. And so a separate women's literature developed. Personal prayers called *tkhines,* dealing with women's concerns, were printed in Yiddish, which is written with Hebrew letters and contains words from German as well as Hebrew and several other languages. These prayers were often written by men, but sometimes by women.

Tkhines included prayers for the health of children, for the safety of a husband during travel, for pregnancy and childbirth, for widows, for recovery from illness, for holidays, and for making contact with, and requests to, the dead.

These prayers raised women's everyday acts in the home, and events of their life cycle, such as childbirth, into the realm of the holy. They were recited individually and voluntarily—unlike men's prayers, which were obligatory.

As Jewish women seek to recover their past, these *tkhines* are being discussed, studied, translated into English, and published. And new prayers continue to be written today, as well as new life-cycle rituals and ceremonies.

As you read about the following women—women you have probably never heard of—try to imagine what their lives were like, what they cared about, and what was important to them.

Rebecca Tiktiner, a Polish woman of the 1500s, wrote about the ethical teachings of famous Jewish sages, and also wrote poetry and prayers. Hers was the first Yiddish book by a woman ever printed.

Sarah Bat Tovim, who lived in the Ukraine in the 1600s, survived in name and legend well beyond her time. Her prayers in a book called *The Three Gates* centered on the traditional commandments for a Jewish woman—baking the Sabbath bread, lighting the Sabbath candles, purifying herself in the *mikvah* or ritual bath—as well as on the holidays, and on images of women in Paradise studying Torah and praising God.

Sarah Rebecca Rachel Leah Horowitz (with all four of the Matriarchs' names in hers!) wrote in Poland in the 1700s. She was an accomplished Talmudic scholar from a well-known rabbinical family. She was concerned with women's prayer, and the role of the Jewish woman.

She wrote a prayer in Yiddish for the Jewish New Year, also called the High Holidays, a time of judgment from on high. Many *tkhines* call upon the matriarchs for help. Hers calls upon the first Matriarch, Sarah. Here is a translation by Chava Weissler, a woman of our time who has studied *tkhines* extensively:

> *First we ask our mother Sarah to . . . pray for our little children that they may not be separated from us. For you know well that it is very bitter when a child is taken away from the mother, as it happened to you. When your son Isaac was taken away from you, it caused you great anguish. And now you have the chance to plead for us.*

Perhaps one of the greatest finds that helps us recover the Jewish woman's past is the autobiography of Glueckel of Hameln, the only full-length autobiography that we know of written by a Jewish woman before the 1800s. Glueckel of Hameln began her work in 1690–91, at the age of forty-six, after her first husband's death. From her book, written in Yiddish, we begin to learn more about the daily life of a Jewish woman from the past and how she felt.

From her journal, we know that Glueckel received an education in a Jewish school for girls in Hamburg, Germany. She was married at age fourteen in Hameln, the German town of Pied Piper fame, and had thirteen children before her husband died. Fortunately, her husband had included Glueckel in all his business decisions, so she was able to run the business after his death.

Addressing her children, she says that she began writing her memoirs "in the hope of distracting my soul from the burdens laid upon it, and the bitter thought that we have lost our faithful shepherd [her husband]. In this way I have managed to live through many wakeful nights, and springing from my bed shortened the sleepless hours."

Alone, Glueckel operated a stocking factory, traded in seed pearls, and attended merchant fairs all over the country, often traveling in uncomfortable wagons down muddy, bumpy roads. She also arranged marriages for her children.

Her diary shows how important her faith was to Glueckel, and how she hoped her children would read her memoirs and be reminded of this faith. She says, "We have our holy Torah in which we may find and learn all that we need for our journey through this world to the world to come. It is like a rope which the great and glorious God has thrown to us as we drown in the stormy sea of life, that we may seize hold of it and be saved."

Glueckel speaks to us from more than three hundred years ago through her diary, showing us what it was like to be Jewish and a woman, a mother and a widow in Germany in the late 1600s. We see that even though women still had no public voice and no vote, they were involved in the economic life of their family. Some wealthy women were also involved in the economic life of their town and country, and had a great deal of responsibility.

We can see that they were *not* invisible in real life, as so many textbooks indicate by their omissions. We can reaffirm their existence, and so reclaim the Jewish woman's past, even as Jewish women re-examine their current role in Judaism. And becoming a bat mitzvah is part of this process.

"IT WAS THE BEGINNING OF THINGS"

···

The Jewish Woman from the 1700s to Modern Times

Events in the next few centuries produced enormous changes in the Western World. After the French Revolution and the rise of industrialization, business and educational opportunities began to open up for both men and women. "Modern" ideas, such as individual rights and the injustice of slavery, took hold.

The home became less and less the center of life. Before industrialization, people often worked at home. Synagogues, houses of study, and the marketplace all were nearby. With the coming of industrialization, people began to work in factories farther away from their homes.

The world was changing and Glueckel of Hameln lived just at the beginning of these changes. Women in general, and Jewish women in particular, could travel more, be heard more, and sometimes even choose not to marry but to pursue their own goals. They began to found organizations for the welfare of the larger community and to run entire organizations by themselves. This helped train women to take roles of leadership in the mixed society of men and women. In the 1900s, they formed unions, organized strikes, fought for the vote and for a greater voice in their religious life.

What had been the role of the Jewish woman for thousands of years was changing. And the few who had set precedents in the centuries before, like Bruriah, and Doña Gracia, and Sarra Coppio Sullam, were being joined by many others. More and more women pushed to be heard through their writings, their actions, their perseverance, abilities, and creativity.

Changes were occurring within Judaism as well as in the world as a whole. One such change was the rise of Hasidism in the late 1700s, a movement which, in its beginnings, was revolutionary and attracted many Jewish women. Inspired by the teachings of the Baal Shem Tov, Hasidism stressed the joy and devotion of the individual, in addition to the study of Torah. Women could express themselves religiously within Hasidism in ways that were not as acceptable in the mainstream Judaism of the times.

Some women, including the Baal Shem Tov's daughter Hodel, became disciples of Hasidic rabbis and spiritual leaders themselves, although this was still more difficult for women than for men. Women such as Menash, daughter of Rabbi Elimelech of Lyzhansk, gave lectures on Hasidic thought. A few even prayed with the prayer shawl called a *tallit* and the prayer boxes called tefillin, which were customarily worn only by men. Some drew people from all over Eastern Europe who came to them for their blessings and guidance.

The most famous female Hasidic spiritual leader was Hannah Rachel Werbermacher, known as the Maid of Ludomir, a controversial figure in her time (1805–92). The daughter of a shopkeeper, she was a very learned woman. Hannah studied and preached, and postponed marriage until the age of forty—unusual for those days. Her disciples built a synagogue for her where she taught Torah to men and women. She eventually settled in the land of Israel. There she studied mysticism and worked to bring about the coming of the messiah, the time of peace.

Women's marital choices were also beginning to change in these years. More and more women and men were deciding on their own mates rather than entering into marriages arranged by their parents. Some women were even choosing not to marry but to pursue a life of community service, or writing, or political activism.

For example, Rachel Morpurgo (1790–1871) chose her own husband. Rachel was from an Italian Jewish family, the Luzzatos, who were well known for their scholarship, and she was allowed to study Torah and Talmud in her home. She may have been the first woman to write and publish modern Hebrew poetry.

Rebecca Gratz (1781–1869) of Philadelphia was born into a well-to-do Jewish family and never married, perhaps because there were only a limited number of available Jewish men of her class. She lived with three brothers and a sister, none of whom married. Rebecca founded the first Jewish Sunday School in America in 1838, the first Jewish foster home in Philadelphia in 1855, and many other associations for the benefit of others. She was the model for the Jewish heroine with the same name in *Ivanhoe* by Sir Walter Scott. Written in the early 1800s, this was a popular historical romance about the time of Richard the Lion Hearted and Robin Hood. These famous figures save Rebecca, daughter of Isaac of York, from being put to death for witchcraft.

Another unmarried woman who influenced many American Jewish women through her writings, urging them to study and learn about Judaism, was the Englishwoman Grace Aguilar (1816–47). One of her novels, *Vale of Cedars*, was about Spanish Jewish Marrano life, Grace's own heritage.

One of the finest Jewish poets of the nineteenth century, admired by Ralph Waldo Emerson, was Emma Lazarus (1849–87), another woman who never married. You might know part of her sonnet "The New Colossus." It is engraved on the base of the Statue of Liberty.

Give me your tired, your poor,

Your huddled masses yearning to breathe free,

The wretched refuse of your teeming shore.

Send these, the homeless, tempest-tost to me.

I lift my lamp beside the golden door!

She wrote this after visiting Wards Island in New York and seeing Jewish refugees from the horrible Russian pogroms of 1881. Through her writing, she worked vigorously to fight against anti-Semitism and for a Jewish homeland. She felt strongly that "until we are all free, we are none of us free."

Being unmarried was one way women could have more freedom to pursue their own interests and careers, although careers for women were still very limited compared to today's opportunities. Many famous women were born into well-to-do families, where they received a good education, and could later afford to pursue volunteer work.

But, of course, not all the Jewish women poets and leaders of the times were unmarried. Nina Davis Salaman (1877–1925), the English poet and translator, was married and the mother of six children. One of her poems, called "Lost Songs," describes the difficulty of trying to have a family and still be creative.

Day by day the sound

Of noisy nothings whirling through their round . . .

Sometimes a thought comes back, and then the pain

Of some lost poem floating on the night

Brings to the heart its inmost song again.

Another great figure of modern times who married is Lady Judith Montefiore (1784–1862) of England. We learn from her diary that she was one of only a handful of European women to visit Palestine in the early nineteenth century. She traveled there with her husband, Sir Moses Montefiore, the first Jew to be knighted. Together they set up self-sufficient farming communities in Palestine, along with a medical dispensary, maternity clinic, girls' school, hospital, and textile factory.

Industrialization had certainly changed things. Many women's lives, whether they married or not, were no longer centered in the home. They were working in the larger society—often in factories and sweatshops. Some of the better-educated and wealthier women, who did not need to work, also stepped out of the spheres of their own homes to create agencies, schools, and clinics for others.

One such woman was Lillian Wald (1867–1910), who was born into a well-to-do middle-class family in Cincinnati. She saw the poverty and needs of the people around her and did something about them. She ran settlement houses in New York and championed child welfare, public health, job training, and education.

And Jewish women, like women in society as a whole, began to organize themselves to effect changes in the world around them. One major step in this direction was the first Congress of Jewish Women, held in 1893 as part of the Parliament of Religions at the Chicago World's Fair. There Hannah Greenbaum Solomon (1858–1942) proposed the formation of the National Council of Jewish Women. This organization was unusual in that it was independent of any religious group led by males.

The president of the New York chapter was Rebekah Bettelheim Kohut (1864–1951), who was born in Hungary and moved to the United States at age two. Her mother had been the first Jewish woman to become a school teacher in Hungary.

Rebekah married Alexander Kohut, a widower with eight children, in 1887. Here was a brave woman, to take on eight children all at once! And little did Rebekah know that only seven years later she would be left a widow to raise these eight children alone. She did this by writing, lecturing, and teaching.

Rebekah wrote her autobiography in two volumes called *My Portion* and *More Yesterdays*. In *More Yesterdays,* she describes the new times for Jewish women of the late 1890s.

> *At the time the Council was founded, participation by women in public life was still a new thing, and there was an excitement, a heady sense of independence, a thrill, a feeling that one was tak-*

ing part in the best kind of revolution, even if it involved nothing more at the moment than parliamentary debates about hot soup and recreation for school children.

People like Hannah Solomon, Rebekah Kohut, and others also attempted to do something about the more controversial problems of their times, like Jewish prostitution and juvenile delinquency, and the problems of the immigrants and the poor. The United States government later funded many of the projects they began.

Jewish women could also join another new organization, Hadassah, founded in 1912. Its first president was Henrietta Szold (1860–1945). Szold, an editor and translator of such works as *The Jewish Encyclopedia,* took her first trip to Palestine in 1909. This trip convinced her of the importance of a Jewish homeland there, and so Hadassah's first major purpose was to provide medical services for Jewish communities in Palestine.

Szold moved to Palestine herself and in 1934 helped found the Youth Aliyah movement, which took Jewish children from Nazi-occupied Europe and brought them to Palestine. In a letter she wrote to her sisters in 1938, Szold said, "It's no use warning me not to overwork; it's no use telling anybody in Palestine to take care. One has to grit one's teeth and take a chance." Szold believed that the survival of the Jewish people depended on creating a homeland in Palestine.

Jewish women were organizing in other ways, too. As early as 1902, in New York City women led a boycott of kosher butcher shops whose meat prices had gone from 12 to 18 cents a pound. News of the boycott appeared in all the New York City newspapers because of the

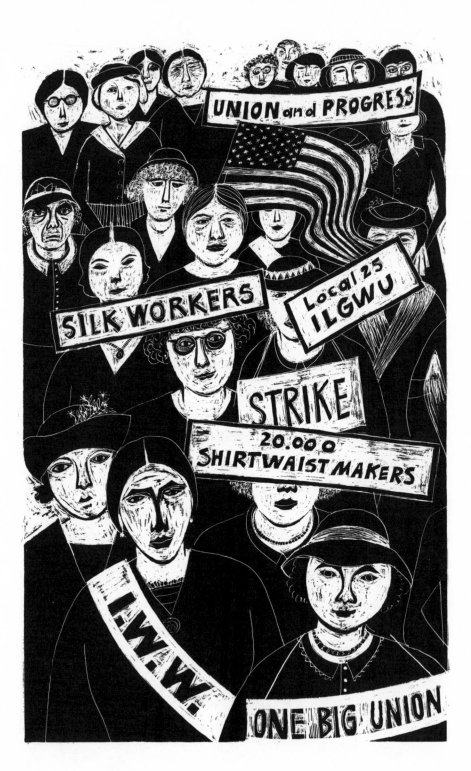

crowds of women in the streets. Middle-aged housewives were arrested after bursting into the shops and throwing meat onto the sidewalks. There were large protest meetings; bail was collected, and leaflets distributed.

Jewish women were also active in forming unions to protect their rights as workers and improve the conditions of the sweatshops. The female shirtwaist makers' strike in 1909 was the largest strike by women in the United States until that time. Jewish women played a large part in the strike. Rose Schneiderman (1882–1972) was one of the first trade union organizers, and Clara Lemlich was a strike organizer.

One of the more colorful and controversial crusaders for unions, as well as many other causes, was Emma Goldman (1869–1940). She was the first woman who dared to teach about birth control practices in public, to show other women that there was an alternative to pregnancy. Laws from the nineteenth century made this an illegal act and so she was jailed in 1916. However, she felt the publicity from her trial was well worth it, as birth control had by now become a national issue.

Women organized to fight for suffrage as well, by going from tenement to tenement to talk about the vote. Henrietta Franklin and Maud Nathan (1862–1946) were two of the Jewish women especially active in this fight for suffrage in the early 1900s. And when women "got the vote," large numbers of Jewish women voted.

Women were demanding an active voice not just in society, but in religion as well. Jewish women wanted to be rabbis and cantors, wanted to have more of a voice in their synagogues by participating

43

in the leading of services and by serving on the board of directors.

These changes, like the vote, took time.

In the early 1920s, just as Judith Kaplan was becoming a bat mitzvah, Jewish women began trying to become rabbis. Martha Neumark took courses in the seminary of the Reform movement, Hebrew Union College. Neumark's desire to be assigned a pulpit for the High Holidays in 1921 forced the Reform movement to consider the ordination of women, which it turned down in 1923. Two more women took coursework, Irma Levy Lindheim in the 1920s at Hebrew Union College, and Helen Hadassah Levinthal in the 1930s at the Jewish Institute of Religion. Both were refused ordination.

Then, in the 1950s, things began to change. When the husband of Paula Ackerman (1893–1989), a rabbi in Meridian, Mississippi, died in 1950, his congregation asked Paula to be their spiritual leader, even though she was not an ordained rabbi. She did this from January 1951 to September 1953 and so was the first female spiritual leader of a mainstream Jewish congregation in the United States.

Paula Ackerman's assumption of her husband's responsibilities after he died reminds us of Glueckel, Benevida Abrabanel, Doña Gracia, and Esther Kiera. However, this time, it wasn't a business that a widow took charge of, but a congregation.

In 1956, women's ordination as rabbis was finally recommended by a committee of the Reform movement. For a long time, no candidates came forward. Then, with the influence of the feminist movement on the way women viewed their role in religious life and in society as a whole, women did begin to apply and were accepted to Hebrew Union College.

Dr. Michael Meyer, Professor of Jewish History at Hebrew Union College, says, "It required a pioneering spirit to be the first woman to go through a male rabbinical seminary, to be ordained and then find a rabbinical position. Sally Preisand was the first to be daring enough." She was ordained in 1972.

The Reconstructionist movement, the one begun by Mordecai Kaplan, Judith's father, began ordaining women in 1973, Sandy Eisenberg Sasso being the first. The Conservative movement agreed in 1983 to allow the ordination of women and ordained their first woman rabbi, Amy Eilberg, in 1985. The Orthodox branch of Judaism still ordains only men.

Women in other religions had an equally difficult time becoming spiritual leaders. One woman I spoke with, who attended divinity school in the south in the 1970s with the intention of becoming an Episcopal priest, found that some of the other students were very intolerant of the idea of a woman being a priest. And although most other mainstream Protestants began ordaining women in the 1950s and 1960s, the Anglican Church in England did not lift its ban on women priests until 1992. Certain other religious movements such as Catholicism and Islam still do not ordain women spiritual leaders.

Rabbi Lynn Gottlieb, spiritual leader of Congregation Nahalat Shalom in Albuquerque, New Mexico, was one of the few women rabbis in the early 1970s. Her first pulpit was with a deaf community in New York in 1973. She remembers how some people would come up to her and say, "Oh, so you're the rabbi of the death community." Her response was, "It's hard to get a living pulpit when you're a woman rabbi!"

Martha Ackelsberg, a Smith College professor, shares her memories of the early 1970s.

A group of about eight of us in the New York havurah [an informal prayer/study group] started a class on women and Judaism. . . . In the end, many of us came to feel that men and women have different experiences of being in the world. If religious tradition is supposed to speak to peoples of very different needs, maybe we should work on how women's differences could be expressed in religious practices and ritual. We knew it could take years to develop these new rituals.

Some friends said we shouldn't just be studying on our own. We should go public. We should do something now to equalize opportunities for women in Judaism.

We gave our study group a name, Ezrat Nashim, which has a double meaning. It means "help for women" and also refers to the area of the ancient Temple that was reserved for women.

Many of us had grown up in the Conservative movement, which had educated us, and now essentially said we couldn't do anything with this education.

We decided to go with a minyan *of ten women to the Conservative movement's Rabbinical Assembly convention in 1971. Our one-page flyer listed our demands, such as being counted in a* minyan, *being admitted to rabbinical school, being called up for* aliyot, *reading from the Torah, and more.*

At first the Rabbinical Assembly said their program was all set. But once we got there, and an article about us appeared in the New York Post *the morning of the conference, the rabbis allowed us to speak.*

We talked to a group of about one hundred rabbis and asked them to take our flyers back to their congregations. In the afternoon, we talked to the rabbis' wives. The programs that had been arranged for them were on flower arranging and subjects like that. Seriously.

We didn't have any idea what the wives' response would be; what they would think of us; what they would say. Maybe they would be angry or uninterested.

After our presentation, an elderly lady, the wife of a prominent rabbi, stood up. To our surprise, she said, "Where have you been all these years?" We felt gratified and invigorated.

It was the beginning of things.

As you can see, the history of bat mitzvah is a direct result of changes in the history of the Jewish woman. As women moved out of the house, as women began to have more of a voice in general society and within Judaism, the possibility of a bat mitzvah ceremony increased. The first bat mitzvah was in 1922, just after women got the vote, but fifty years before there were any women rabbis.

And most Jewish girls were not as fortunate as Judith Kaplan. The majority did not have an opportunity to become a bat mitzvah in a synagogue ceremony until the 1950s or later.

Now a bat mitzvah ceremony is often the same as a bar mitzvah in Reform, Reconstructionist, and most Conservative synagogues. Some

Orthodox synagogues are offering variations of a bat mitzvah ceremony.

Because of the changing role of women in Judaism, the bat mitzvah ceremony is really quite new, and still evolving. Today many women who could not have a bat mitzvah ceremony when they were thirteen are having one as adults. Sometimes they choose to do this in groups whose members have studied together all year.

In 1992, seventy years after her bat mitzvah ceremony in 1922, Judith Kaplan Eisenstein celebrated with a second ceremony at age eighty-two. This time, she was actually called up to the Torah, and she read from the holy Torah scroll. Seventy years before, it had been her father who read from the scroll while Judith was seated at a distance from the Torah and read her part from a bound Bible. In this span of seventy years, women's lives in many ways, and specifically in religion, had changed greatly.

So while you stand before the congregation and chant the Hebrew blessings or read your speech, or while you sit in one of the front rows watching your friend do this, think of all these women in the past—of the Matriarchs, the Deborahs and Esthers, the Rebecca Gratzes, the Rebekah Kohuts, and the Judith Kaplans. Think of this long history of brave and courageous women, many of whom could not be mentioned here because of lack of space, or because we do not know enough about them. They would certainly be amazed and gratified to see what girls and women are doing today.

PART TWO

··

CEREMONY AND CELEBRATION

DON'T FORGET TO STUDY

Preparation

DIFFERENT KINDS OF JEWS,
DIFFERENT KINDS OF CEREMONIES

Preparation for a bat mitzvah ceremony depends partly on the desires and beliefs of the bat mitzvah and her family. It also depends on where she is going to have the ceremony and what the rabbi or leader requires. There is a lot of variation in what a bat mitzvah may do.

One of the reasons for this variation is that there are different kinds of Jews. To begin with, there are four major groups within Judaism, just as there are different kinds of Christians such as Catholics and Episcopalians, Lutherans and Baptists, and so on. The Jewish movements are Reform, Orthodox, Conservative, and Reconstructionist. There are also Jews who do not consider themselves as any of these. And there are groups of Jews who have formed *havurot,* informal groups that pray and celebrate in members' homes, with or without a rabbi, and develop their own styles of worship. There are also Jews who are more secular than religious: They approach Judaism from a more cultural, communal, or historical orientation.

Generally, members of the Orthodox movement accept the Torah, both Written and Oral, as God given. The Oral Torah is made up of those laws and commentaries handed down through thousands of years by the rabbis. Orthodox Jews believe that these laws and teachings are to be strictly observed and can be changed only by Orthodox rabbinical authority.

Reform Judaism arose in Germany in response to changing times, the challenges of the emancipation and enlightenment that began at the end of the eighteenth century. This movement considers basic Jewish values to be eternal, but recognizes the right of individual Jews to make educated choices about their religious practice. Reform Jewish practice may vary from place to place and has undergone constant change over the decades since its beginnings.

The Conservative movement began soon after the Reform movement, in the middle of the 1800s. Its early leaders felt that some changes in Jewish practice were inevitable, but made these changes only with great reluctance. Conservative Jews today follow decisions about changes made by the Conservative rabbinical body, called the Rabbinical Assembly.

And remember Judith Kaplan? It was her father, Rabbi Mordecai Kaplan, who began Reconstructionist Judaism in the 1900s, although it was not his intention to form a separate movement. Rabbi Kaplan saw Judaism in America as an "evolving religious civilization" which would touch every aspect of an American Jew's life.

Because of the differences in philosophy of the various movements, there have been differences in the way the bat mitzvah ceremony has taken shape within each movement. However, these differences are less important than the fact that leaders and lay people in each movement have come to recognize the significance of publicly affirming a Jewish girl's coming of age.

Within Reform, Reconstructionist, and most Conservative congregations and *havurot,* a girl will most likely have the same kind of ceremony that a boy has for his coming of age. Most of these ceremonies take place in a synagogue, in conjunction with the reading of the Torah, which is traditionally done on Monday, Thursday, and Shabbat (Sabbath) mornings and afternoons, *Rosh Hodesh* (the New Moon), and certain holidays.

In the past, Orthodox communities did not encourage a bat mitzvah ceremony in a synagogue sanctuary. They would (and still do) sometimes have a party at home or in the synagogue social hall, where the bat mitzvah would give a *Dvar Torah,* a talk based on the weekly Torah reading. But things have been changing within the Orthodox community, and some communities now celebrate the bat mitzvah ceremony on Sunday in a synagogue sanctuary where the girl chants a haftarah, a reading from the Prophets, and gives a speech.

Some Orthodox families choose instead to have a bat mitzvah ceremony on Shabbat morning in a women's prayer group. Here the girls lead part of the synagogue service and read from the Torah, and also chant the haftarah and deliver a speech. At these services, no more than nine men are permitted to be present, and they sit behind the *mehitzah,* the separating curtain. This is because, traditionally, a minimum of ten men constitutes the religious quorum required for certain prayers and rituals. If there were ten men present—a *minyan*—a man would have to lead the services, and the women would have to sit behind the *mehitzah*.

Rabbi Yosef Kanefsky, associate rabbi at the (Orthodox) Hebrew Institute of Riverdale, explains that

> *because the public role of the Jewish women was so minimal for thousands of years, the notion of a public coming-into-the-adult-community ceremony was something no one would ever have conceived of. So the degree to which a particular congregation will embrace the bat mitzvah ceremony will correlate directly to the degree they accept the idea that women should play a public [rather than home-based] role in the Jewish community. There is a wide variety of ceremonies and celebrations within the Orthodox movement, including not celebrating a bat mitzvah.*

His synagogue does have a woman's prayer group where girls may do virtually the same things that a boy does. Rabbi Kanefsky senses that "there is a strong feeling of sisterhood at these events and the girl really enters not only the adult community, but the adult Jewish woman's community."

In interviewing girls who have become *bnot mitzvah* (plural of bat mitzvah), I found that some girls' families are a mixture of different kinds of Jews, and not clearly identified with one movement or another. One girl was from a family she called "Conservadox." Her father is Orthodox and her mother is Conservative. This family

reached a compromise at the girl's coming of age by having the ceremony in a Conservative synagogue that had egalitarian services where
women and men have equal access to leadership roles. They had an
all-women-led service, so that only women were up at the *bimah*, the
platform from which the Torah is read. There were also no micro-
phones, which the Orthodox do not allow on the Sabbath. But the
father did agree to mixed seating of men and women in the sanctuary,
and to more than nine men being present in the congregation.

Some families are mixed in another way, with one parent who is
Jewish and one who isn't. One girl I interviewed said her mom, who
isn't Jewish, felt a little left out. "My dad could help me, but my mom
didn't know Hebrew. She didn't have the experience of bat mitzvah
or Hebrew school. She did come up on the *bimah* with my father. And
she did help me with my Dvar Torah. Overall, it was okay. I think she
enjoyed it. She just didn't get to take as big a part as my dad did."

This family belonged to a Reform synagogue which encouraged
some participation by non-Jewish parents. Different congregations in
the different movements involve a non-Jewish parent in different
ways. And some do not allow participation of a non-Jewish parent in
the bat mitzvah ceremony at all.

As we can see from this discussion of different kinds of ceremonies,
it is natural to model the bat mitzvah ceremony on the coming-of-age
ceremony for boys. However, there are some people who question
whether a girl should or would want to have the same ceremony as a
boy, just adopting the male model without question. They say that
girls and women may want to invent their own ceremonies and customs with the help of parents and teachers. Or they may want to add

their own innovations, themes, prayers, and talents to the already existing model.

Same or Different?

Cherie Koller-Fox has been exploring this issue for more than twenty years. As a Jewish educator in the 1970s, she worked with a group of girls to design ritual clothing objects they could wear on the day of their becoming *bnot mitzvah* that would be different from the boys' ritual clothing—that would reflect their own ideas about who they were as young Jewish women. They agreed on a headband embroidered with a verse from the Bible or the prayer book instead of a *kippah* (skullcap), and a self-designed and decorated jacket in place of a *tallit* (prayer shawl).

Cherie Koller-Fox, who is now a rabbi, says:

When I worked with that group of girls in the 1970s, we were just at the beginning of the women's movement. In that particular synagogue where I worked, girls had no women role models. They didn't see women on the bimah *and girls had never worn a* tallit *before.*

We started out in the 1970s trying to find our way and we have found we belong where the boys and men are. A girl doesn't have a different responsibility as a Jewish adult, so we bring her into the adult community in the same way as a boy. There are other rituals we can do differently as women and girls, such as baby namings, and ceremonies to mark menstruation and menopause, other moments that are good for reclaiming who we

are as Jewish women. At those moments, it feels right to surround
girls with women (and boys with men) for their special rituals.

Most girls aren't interested in doing their bat mitzvah differ-
ently from a boy's ceremony. They're feminists. They want to do
what is to be done. There are *subtle differences for the girls and*
boys, such as in the color and design of their tallit *and* kippah,
and in some of the readings the families choose.

Some people working with students who are becoming *bnot mitz-*
vah emphasize honoring the individual student, whether that student
is male or female. Of course, the students' gender may influence what
they want their ceremony and celebration to be like. But any individual student may have ideas and desires different from others.

Shonna Husbands-Hankin, a Judaic artist who creates Jewish ritual objects, including silk *tallitot,* says this about honoring the individual. "Let twelve- and thirteen-year-olds shape their coming of age as
much as possible so this time of their life will reflect what's true for
them."

About her daughter Talya's experience, Shonna says:

Talya celebrated twice. The first time was in Jerusalem at Hul-
dah's Gate, the gate to the Temple Mount on the south.

Beforehand, we created a tallit *and painted a picture of the*
old city of Jerusalem and the pathway to Huldah's Gate on it.
Talya chose the colors and the imagery for the painting. We
mailed the tallit *to different friends and family so they could tie*
three of the four corners with tzitziyot, *the ritual fringes. Then*

they mailed the tallit *back to us, and as a family, we tied the fringes on the fourth corner. In this way, friends' and family's energy is with Talya when she wears her* tallit.

At home in Eugene, Oregon, for the second bat mitzvah ceremony, in May of 1993, Talya wanted to be outside and near moving water. They found a meadow near a river ten minutes from home and the synagogue. "We wanted to honor Talya and her wishes," says Shonna. "And because of the weather, we weren't sure where the ceremony would be up until that very morning. It was a foggy morning."

They went ahead with the outdoor ceremony and set up chairs in a semicircle. They brought the Torah to the meadow, with birds singing and peacocks strutting around.

They had cut and pasted eighty pages to form their own prayer book for their Shabbat morning service. In addition to prayers, they included readings from here and there, poetry and songs which Talya helped to choose. After Talya chanted from the Torah and the haftarah, all her friends ran up to her and gave her flowers and hugged her. And when the service was over, the guests put her in a chair, lifted her high, and danced with her in the meadow.

"SOMETHING FROM THE INSIDE, NOT FROM THE OUTSIDE": THE TUTOR

With all the variety and choices within Judaism, what will a girl most likely do at her bat mitzvah ceremony and how will she do it?

First of all, she will probably need a tutor. Usually the rabbi or prin-

cipal of the synagogue Hebrew school has a list of possibilities. Because this tutor will guide her through about six months or even a full year of intensive study and training, it is important that the tutor be someone she can relate to.

Rachel Diamond says, "I had a good tutor. I had a lot of choices. There were ten different ones on the rabbi's list. I wanted someone I would be comfortable singing in front of every week."

Sher Sweet, who became a bat mitzvah as an adult, says of her tutor, her rabbi, "He was a lot like a midwife. He was not too directive, but let me make many of the decisions. I got so much from my interaction with him. When the rabbi said I could do a lot more at my ceremony than I had planned, I said, 'Oh, no!' But I ended up doing it because of his encouragement."

Hanna Tiferet Siegel is a singer, songwriter, liturgical artist and teacher. She has also been a bar and bat mitzvah tutor since the late 1970s, and says, "It is important to have a teacher to inspire you to understand what you're doing. That way you will be learning from the inside, as well as from the outside."

It is important to remember that the preparation period is not only about learning to chant for the performance on the *bimah*. The emphasis should really be on the person chanting—who she is, and who she is becoming.

This preparation period is really about growing up—becoming a responsible and dedicated member of a community—and about taking on new responsibilities. It is about finding out what is expected of a Jewish adult. It is about having more power in the things we do. The tutor plays a big role in this whole process.

A future bat mitzvah usually meets with her tutor once a week. The tutor often prepares a tape of the Hebrew blessings, the Torah portion, and the haftarah for the student. The tutor helps the girl write a speech in English and, if she is to lead part of the services, may help with that as well. The bat mitzvah is expected to practice on her own between tutoring sessions. Therefore, each bat mitzvah has extra homework on top of an already busy middle schooler's schedule!

When a future bat mitzvah begins her tutoring, it is assumed that she has been enrolled in a Hebrew school for several years, and has been attending one, two, or three times a week. There she will have learned something about Jewish ethics, holidays, commandments, prayer, history, and the Hebrew language.

Sometimes a future bat mitzvah begins the process later. In this case, she would expect to study with a tutor longer than the usual period, in order to learn about her religion and to read Hebrew.

I HAVE TO SING?: CHANTING

The Blessings

The future bat mitzvah usually learns the blessings recited before and after the reading of the Torah, and the blessings said before and after the reading of the haftarah. These are chanted to age-old melodies passed down through the generations.

When a person goes up to the *bimah* to chant the blessings for the Torah reading, she is being called up for an *aliyah* (plural, *aliyot*), which means "going up." This is considered a great honor.

To give you some idea of the sounds of these Hebrew blessings,

61

here are the first few Hebrew words transliterated—that is, written with English letters:

Barkhu et Adonai ha-m'vorakh

These words mean "Bless God, the One Who is to be praised."

These blessings are usually printed in big letters (in Hebrew and/or transliteration) on a card on the *bimah*, so anyone going up for an *aliyah* will be able to recite the words. The bat mitzvah isn't the only one who might get flustered and need a crib sheet!

Often synagogues honor the parents and other members of the bat mitzvah's family with an *aliyah* at the ceremony. Depending on the synagogue, there may be as many as eight of these honors, seven plus the bat mitzvah. This accounts for some of the comings and goings of different people to the *bimah*.

Besides praising God, these particular blessings praise and thank God for giving the Torah to the Jews. The idea here—that the Jews were chosen to receive the Torah—points to a Jew's obligation to carry out the commandments of the Torah, to accept the lifelong responsibility of living by Jewish values and ethics. The word *chosen* is in no way intended to mean that Jews are better than others.

The blessings chanted before the haftarah praise God for the prophets who reminded the ancient Israelites (as well as us today) of God's truths. The blessings chanted after the haftarah continue to praise and thank God, and ask that God bring us joy and a time of great peace. The blessings end with thanks for the Sabbath day, *this day*, one of rest, prayer, holiness, and celebration.

The Torah Reading

The Five Books of Moses are the first five books of the Hebrew Bible: Genesis, Exodus, Leviticus, Numbers, and Deuteronomy.

Genesis contains many famous Bible stories. It begins with the creation and ends with the death of Joseph of the coat-of-many-colors fame in Egypt.

The Book of Exodus describes the Israelites' slavery in Egypt, and the Exodus, the departure of the slaves from Egypt; the giving of the Ten Commandments and making the golden calf, the golden idol these former slaves bowed down to in the desert.

Leviticus tells of the Priestly rituals and holiness code, including the sacrifices; Numbers, of the wanderings in the wilderness after the Exodus; and Deuteronomy, of various laws, and more about Moses.

In the synagogue, it takes a whole year to read the entire Torah scroll. (The Jewish year is based on a different calendar system from the secular year. The years are reckoned according to the moon and the sun, but the months according to the moon.) The Torah is not read every single day of the week, but only on Monday, Thursday, and Saturday mornings, Saturday afternoons, *Rosh Hodesh* (the first day, sometimes two days, of a new month), holidays, and fast days. Some congregations read only one third of the scroll a year. They read the entire scroll over a three-year period.

The Five Books of Moses, the Torah, are divided into weekly portions, each called a *parashah*. The bat mitzvah is assigned a particular *parashah*. A bat mitzvah will often learn to chant part of the *parashah*. In traditional synagogues, it is usually the *maftir*, which is the last part of the Torah read on a particular day. But she may choose to read more than one section.

Rabbi Lynn Gottlieb of Albuquerque, New Mexico, has been tutoring future *bnai mitzvah* (plural for bar mitzvah, as well as bar and bat mitzvah together) since the 1970s. She prefers to have her students learn to chant a larger section than only the *maftir* directly from the ancient scroll, the Torah. Most often, the main part of what the future bar or bat mitzvah learns to chant is a haftarah, a portion from the Prophets, and this chanting is learned from a tape. The haftarah will not be read directly from the ancient Torah scroll, but from a printed booklet or book. Rabbi Gottlieb says, "Why give them only three lines of Torah? It is more powerful to chant directly from the ancient scroll, from the heart of the matter."

Rabbi Gottlieb, along with many others, worries about the "cassette recording syndrome," where the bat or bar mitzvah's preparation period is mainly one of memorizing long sections of chanted Hebrew from a casette tape, bonding more with the tape than anything else.

Trop

To avoid this syndrome, some future *bnot mitzvah* learn to sing the Torah and haftarah portions by learning a system of musical notation called *trop*. Students who learn the *trop* system are not so dependent on their cassette tapes: in fact, they do not even need a tape. They can figure out how their haftarah should sound by applying the *trop* system.

If you look at a page of Torah or haftarah text in a *Humash*—a book with the Five Books of Moses plus the *haftarot* in it used during the Torah service—you will see funny shapes above and below the letters, little semicircles, jagged lines, and dots. These *trop* marks are musical notes telling how to sing the syllables of the words. Each sign represents a certain melodic sound or group of sounds in a particular *trop* system.

Complications

What can be confusing is that not all *trop* systems are the same, since these have been handed down for almost three thousand years, in countries all over the world. Also, the Torah uses a different system of singing the squiggles from the one in the haftarah reading!

There are a few more things that make reading from the Torah such a challenge. There are no vowel marks written under or next to the letters, no punctuation marks, and no *trop* signs in the Torah itself!

Reading directly from the Torah scroll would be like reading English without *a, e, i, o,* or *u.* The words *Sabbath, haftarah* and *Torah* would look like this: *Sbbth, hftrh,* and *Trh.*

The Hebrew vowel system changed long ago, but the Torah is still written according to the old system. Scribes in each generation ever since have been careful to copy each scroll exactly as the last was written.

Therefore, a bat mitzvah must memorize the vowels and *trop* of her Torah reading, if she is to read directly out of the Torah scroll on her special day. She learns to read first from the *Humash* or from a booklet with vowels and *trop* signs printed on the pages. Then she learns to read from a book called a *tikkun,* which shows how the words will look in the Torah scroll without the vowels and *trop* signs.

The system of musical and phonetic notation that appears in

printed versions of the Torah such as the *Humash,* although not in the actual handwritten Torah scroll, was developed by scholars before the tenth century. They organized a system of vowel points so readers could pronounce the words properly, and a system of musical signs so they could sing the words to the traditional ancient melodies.

The fact that the Torah is always written by hand makes it more difficult to read. Each scroll's calligraphy looks slightly different, though the words themselves are the same. This is why it is best for the bat mitzvah, after she has learned to chant from the printed *Humash* page or from her booklet, to practice with the actual Torah scroll she will read from at her ceremony. She can arrange to do this with her tutor or rabbi. The motto is: The fewer surprises, the better.

The bat mitzvah will read the haftarah, however, from a printed book and not from a handwritten scroll, so this part will not be quite as difficult as the Torah reading. But now you can see one reason that all this preparation and tutoring begins many months before the big day!

Haftarah

Haftarah means "conclusion" or "completion" in English, as it completes the Torah service. Each Sabbath has its particular Torah portion, and also its particular haftarah. (If the coming-of-age ceremony is on a Monday or Thursday morning, Shabbat afternoon, or *Rosh Hodesh*, there will be no haftarah, but only the Torah reading.)

The haftarah is selected from the books of the Prophets, many of whose names you may recognize, such as Isaiah, Jeremiah, Ezekiel, Amos. These *haftarot* (plural for haftarah) have some connection to the Torah reading of that week. They may mention one of the people or holidays or themes of that particular Torah reading.

The Torah and haftarah readings are usually all chanted, as are the blessings, so that a bat mitzvah does quite a lot of "singing" on her special day.

My own daughter, Josee, was worried about this. She says, "I thought everybody would laugh at me. Someone once told me I had a bad voice. I was so relieved when it was over. Getting up in front of all those people, people I knew and people I didn't know, and having to sing was one of the scariest things about it all. But no one laughed. And I wished I could have gotten back up and done it again."

AND TALK TOO!: THE *DVAR TORAH*

Learning all this chanting, however, is not all the preparation a bat mitzvah must do for her ceremony. She often delivers a *Dvar Torah,* a speech in English discussing her Torah and haftarah portions, and how they are meaningful for her today.

This custom is quite old. For the past two hundred years, *bnot* as well as *bnai mitzvah* have given speeches as part of their coming-of-age ceremonies. This is to show that they understand the teachings of Judaism and know how to apply them to contemporary life. This custom of a twelve-year-old girl giving a talk to mark her coming of age preceded the first bat mitzvah ceremony in 1922 by more than a hundred years. As early as the 1800s, some families in countries such as France and Italy were celebrating their daughter's twelfth birthday with a festive meal called a *seudat mitzvah.* The daughter would often give a talk at this meal.

Help in writing this speech can come from the tutor, rabbi, and parents. Ayana Morse says, "I had the speech all worked out. My dad came over and said he thought of my *parashah* in a different way than I had written about it in my speech. He told me what he thought. I ended up changing the speech just a week before my ceremony! Actually, I liked it better, but I didn't want to tell my father that and admit he was right!"

When Hanna Tiferet Siegel works with a future bat mitzvah on her speech, she highlights any women who appear in the Torah portion or haftarah, and explores their presence as deeply as possible. She asks, "What about the women?" She tries to give women a voice.

One of her students, Ayala Danya Galton, chanted the haftarah from the Biblical book of Judges that is about Jephthah. Before going into battle, Jephthah promises God that if he is victorious, he will sacrifice whatever comes out of the door of his house to meet him on his return. After his victory, it is his daughter who comes out to greet him.

Ayala discussed this haftarah in her speech and asked some questions. "What was the name of Jephthah's daughter? Was she truly sacrificed or did she become something like a priestess?" Ayala also writes, "If Jephthah's daughter could speak to us today, what would she say? Do you have any ideas?"

After sharing some of her own ideas, Ayala ends with, "While I was thinking about what Jephthah's daughter might say, I realized how lucky I am to be alive and to become a bat mitzvah."

My daughter Josee's haftarah was from the portion called *Naso,* which tells the story of Samson's birth—Samson of long-hair-and-great-strength fame.

Josee was disturbed by the fact that Samson's father had a name in the haftarah, Manoah, but his mother's name was left out. So in her speech, Josee said, "I'm going to give Samson's mother a name, Emunah, which means faith. She had so much faith that when the angel came up to her and told her she would have a son after all these years, she believed the angel. I wonder—if she didn't have faith, would Samson have been born at all? I think faith has a lot to do with miracles."

Shonna Husbands-Hankin says of her daughter Talya's speech:

Talya's Torah portion was about making offerings. So remembering her trip to Israel, she talked about honoring diversity in Judaism. About how going to Israel and loving it for all its diversity is one of life's greatest offerings.

On the holiday of Shavuot, she had been at the Western Wall in Jerusalem with the Orthodox. Then we went to a kibbutz to celebrate the holiday there, where the first fruit offerings were made—a very different sort of celebration. That day clearly showed the diversity in Israel, and Talya used her experience as an example.

Not all *bnot mitzvah* give what we think of as a speech. Some may act out the *parashah*, costume and all. And others may give another kind of presentation to explain their section of Torah and haftarah.

"IT'S ABOUT COURAGE": INDIVIDUAL TALENTS

I talked with tutors who encourage their students to bring their individual talents to their coming-of-age ceremonies.

Rabbi Lynn Gottlieb has a background in theater. When she played the Wicked Witch of the West in *The Wizard of Oz* as an eighth grader in Allentown, Pennsylvania, she got a standing ovation for the melting scene! Rabbi Gottlieb says: "Theater gives kids a tremendous confidence in themselves which I now make part of my training of students. I encourage them to explore different voices inside themselves and act out different roles and parts. I allow them to be articulate, to play with the tradition, to be funny and serious, and to explore their questions in relation to the tradition."

One student was so shy that Rabbi Gottlieb would make tea by herself in the kitchen to get the girl to talk louder from the next room. "She was a whisperer," the rabbi says.

Rabbi Gottlieb noticed that one time this student was unusually quiet. Finally, the girl asked her, "Do you think my bat mitzvah could be funny?"

"What do you have in mind?" said Rabbi Gottlieb.

It turned out that the student was wondering if she could do stand-up comedy at her bat mitzvah ceremony. She took out books about Jewish humor from the library and made up a character—Zetch the Kvetch. She created a mask and told all her relatives that an old woman was coming from Israel to visit.

She incorporated themes from her *parashah* into a twenty-minute monologue which she delivered during her ceremony. The monologue told what it was like to leave Egypt with Moses, who didn't have a sense of humor. ("That's why we formed a comedy club!") And a little brother who, every hour of every day for forty years, asked, "Are we there yet?"

Rabbi Gottlieb says, "This bat mitzvah transformed her and gave her a lot of confidence. She's still doing comedy and writing in high school. And this character has come back to synagogue on Passover, and other holidays.

"This girl was supported by her family. I see it as part of my job to get the family behind the efforts of the student. It's also part of my job to listen to what the student wants to do and to participate in the process, rather than to say: This is your assigned part."

One student with artistic talent did a painting of the seventh day of creation, which was mentioned in her *parashah*. She put the painting on the *bimah*, read from her portion, and talked about the painting at her ceremony.

Another girl enjoyed writing. At her ceremony, she read a piece of historical fiction she had written about a girl who became a bat mitzvah in secret in a basement during the Holocaust.

Rabbi Gottlieb says, "The people who come to these ceremonies really get to know the bat mitzvah. And the guests from outside the community can't believe what these kids can do."

Hanna Tiferet Siegel also looks to bring out the uniqueness of each of her students. Sometimes she has tutored students who believed they couldn't sing or who were dyslexic. Hanna never believes they can't do it. She has seen the students' abilities grow.

She says, "The whole process is about courage. Sometimes their ability is not as developed in a certain area. So I encourage his or her strengths and suggest new possibilities. I don't take his or her limitations at face value. I explore to see if there really *is* a 'limitation' or if it is only fear. I believe in my students. That's important. How many people take that kind of an interest in you in your life?"

Part of her work with the students is an "in-depth exploration of the *Shema,*" one of the most important Jewish prayers, which begins by proclaiming the Oneness of God. The students "grapple with the theological question of who God is for them, and how Judaism will be a part of their lives." What they write is shared at the ceremony with the guests.

Sonia Rebecca Scherr wrote this about the *Shema* in her talk. "For me, the *Shema* is a very personal prayer. Often, when I need to make a difficult decision, find myself in an uncomfortable situation, or do the thing I know is right even if it is an unpopular choice, I say the *Shema*. It guides me, calms me, comforts me, and helps me enter the situation with greater strength and wisdom."

She says the *Shema* "asks us to take care of God's creation, for every creation, no matter how small, is precious—and fragile. It warns us that, unlike Adam and Eve, we will not be given a second chance. We live in the last and only Garden. The message tells us that yes, we *are* the Earth's keepers. Within each of us we have the power to destroy, or save, God's greatest creation of all—our planet."

One of Hanna's most memorable experiences tutoring was with two friends who wanted to have a double ceremony. Hanna says, "One girl was very intellectual and the other was artistic. They did an original play based on their haftarah. I was moved by how their friendship overcame their differences."

Another approach, developed by Rabbi Kenneth R. Berger in the 1970s, emphasizes a creative project which the future bar or bat mitzvah chooses. The project may involve a mulitmedia creation like a diorama, or a crafted or cooked creation, like a *tallit* or a hallah, the braided bread for the Sabbath. There are endless possibilities.

The students present their project to the congregation at their ceremony, as well as their opinions about and reactions to their topic, and the experience of working with it. One topic chosen was Hannah Senesh, a Jewish woman paratrooper who went on a rescue mission behind Nazi lines in World War II. She was captured by the Germans in 1944 and executed. Another student chose to learn more about the Sephardic Jewish community, the Jews who originally came from Spain and Portugal, and another chose the similarities between Earth Day and the Jewish holiday of the trees called *Tu B'Shvat*.

Sylvia Avner, a synagogue librarian, also found that individual projects chosen and executed by future *bnai mitzvah* were most meaningful. One student created three marionettes, Manoah, Mrs. Manoah (or

Emunah, as Josee named her), and the Messenger, to act out her haftarah, *Naso*. She presented the show to Hebrew school classes. Another created a miniature Temple with objects inside all built to scale, which was put on display the week before the bat mitzvah ceremony.

"GIVING AND NOT JUST GETTING": THE EMPHASIS ON MITZVAH

Also part of the preparation for becoming a bat mitzvah today is the emphasis on the word *mitzvah,* commandment. Performing commandments or *mitzvot* (plural of *mitzvah*), and accepting responsibility, is part of becoming a Jewish adult, as seen in the phrase itself. Bar or bat mitzvah literally means "one who is subject to or responsible for the commandment," one who has the obligation of fulfilling commandments.

Many synagogue programs and tutors are requiring students to learn about and perform *mitzvot* in the months leading up to the actual ceremony. Hanna Tiferet Siegel uses a program called "*Mitzvot and Me*" to teach her students that they are giving, as well as getting. Many future *bnai mitzvah* work in soup kitchens, visit the sick in hospitals, or collect food for food banks.

Danny Siegel, an author, lecturer, and poet finds people he calls "*mitzvah* heroes" who serve as an inspiration for others. One bat mitzvah heroine is Elana Erdstein. Elana collected unused samples of soaps, shampoo, and other personal items from local hotels and corporations and anyone else she could think of for her *mitzvah* project. She donated these to a local homeless center, a battered women's shelter, and a home for troubled teens.

At first, she thought if she tried hard, she'd get a thousand pieces. But by the time of her bat mitzvah ceremony, she had collected twenty-five thousand items! She was even invited to a dental convention where she told about her project from the podium and was provided then and there with toothbrushes and dental floss.

Among other things that Elana learned from her experience was the fact that "you can buy caviar with food stamps, but not toothpaste."

Also, future *bnot mitzvah* are taking seriously the recommendation to give part of their gifts to *tzedakah,* usually defined as charity. Actually *tzedakah* means something a little different from charity. It means justice and is an obligation, not a whim. In other words, one doesn't give only when one feels the urge, but whenever there is a need. Jewish law recommends giving between 10 and 20 percent of one's income and gifts to *tzedakah*. Being able to give *tzedakah* to a cause of her own choosing is often a powerful and positive feeling for a bat mitzvah.

When you go to a bat mitzvah ceremony, you may be given a program booklet that tells where the bat mitzvah has decided to contribute. Or you may see something like this on the invitation: "When you come to the reception, please bring a warm coat you no longer need. We will be donating these to the survival center." One bat mitzvah had her invitations printed on the back of cards which said that she had donated the money for a tree to be planted in Israel in honor of that guest.

Elaina Deutsch decorated the tables at her party with books, which were later donated to local libraries. Her party theme was "Great Books" and each table was named for its book. A bookplate in the front of the book listed all the guests at that table, and said that the book was being donated in their honor.

All this work of learning about what it truly means to become an adult, to take on responsibility, and to care about others begins in the preparation period. It goes on behind the scenes, and before the actual ceremony. And, we hope, after, too.

CHOOSING YOUR OWN WORDS: BOOKLETS

Yet another area for a bat mitzvah to explore, take part in, and leave her mark on, is the planning and printing of a booklet to be used by congregants and guests at the ceremony. These are sometimes as simple as a little flyer explaining the ceremony and service, with a short message from the bat mitzvah. Others are more elaborate, with copies of the Torah portion and haftarah that the bat mitzvah will be reading.

Sometimes, the bat mitzvah has chosen a theme for her special day, such as peace or ecology or growing up. Then the booklet may include poems, prayers, and stories on this theme that will be read at certain points during the service. The more the bat mitzvah can be involved in her ceremony, in this way and in others, the more meaningful her experience will be.

One booklet included poems and writings of some famous Jewish women such as the poet Emma Lazarus; the young diarist of the Holocaust, Anne Frank; and artist Judy Chicago, who has encouraged women to use female imagery and subjects in their artwork.

Another booklet carefully outlined the family tree of both sides of the bat mitzvah's family.

Still another booklet contained the bat mitzvah's drawing and prayers for peace, and a tribute to her grandfather who had just died. On the cover of this particular booklet was a photo of her as a baby, and of her as she is now.

A different booklet, produced by a family that is very much involved in Yiddish culture, included a poem in Yiddish with an English translation. The bat mitzvah's grandmother read this poem during the service.

A booklet may also be useful if the bat mitzvah and her family want to change the wording of a prayer book to make its language nonsexist. For instance, in her ceremony, Sher Sweet referred to God as both "He" and "She," so the God language wouldn't be exclusively male or female. Some people prefer to use the general names of God, such as "The Holy One," and avoid the personal pronouns *he* and *she* altogether. The bat mitzvah's booklet may also include nonsexist readings, prayers, and prayer translations to balance a prayer book that does not use nonsexist language.

Some families and *bnot mitzvah* are also designing their own invitations as well as their own booklets, producing these on home computers or using local printing shops.

Innovations such as choosing your own words for invitations and booklets personalize the coming-of-age ceremony and are all part of the reexamination of women's role in Judaism.

BECOMING A WOMAN: A POWERFUL TRANSITION

Rabbi Sandy Eisenberg Sasso says that those working with *bnai mitzvah* must not forget the powerful transition through which these students are passing. "Children who are for the first time wrapping their arms in tefillin are also using deodorant for the first time. Those who are choosing an appropriate *tallit* may also be choosing, with great interest, the correct size bra."

Hanna Tiferet Siegel says of this transition period, "I try to acknowledge that my student is becoming a man or a woman, physically, emotionally, and spiritually. I would really like to tie bat mitzvah in with this by doing ceremonies with the girls and the community of adult women as the girls begin their periods. That way they can feel their connection to the moon, and inner and outer cycles. The boys would meet with men and do things that empower them as men."

Empowering girls as they grow to be women, and boys as they grow to be men, during this coming-of-age time has been a goal in the religious rites of many cultures. This empowerment lies behind the Jewish ceremony as well. Across the country, Jewish educators and leaders are adding some kind of preceremony initiation to the preparation for the bat or bar mitzvah.

Rabbi Lynn Gottlieb has developed specific initiation ceremonies for *bnai mitzvah*. Once a year, she introduces future *bnot mitzvah* as a group into the *Rosh Hodesh* community of Jewish women with a special ceremony. The *Rosh Hodesh* community is an ongoing group who meet once a month at the time of the new moon. They welcome the new moon, which coincides with the new Jewish month, with rituals, prayers, and ceremonies.

Rosh Hodesh means "head of the month" and is traditionally a semi-holiday for women. It commemorates that time long ago in the desert when the people waited for Moses to come down from the mountain. They waited and waited until, impatient, they began to build a god they could see, an idol, a golden calf. But according to legend, the women refused to help, refused to give up their jewelry for the making of the golden idol. And so the rabbis later honored them with this monthly day of rest from work.

The emphasis in Rabbi Gottlieb's initiation ritual is on the spiritual aspects of what it means to become a woman, with some relationship to the physical, since many, though by no means all of the girls, have begun to menstruate by this age.

Rabbi Gottlieb also takes groups of future *bnot mitzvah* on their own initiation ritual. Often this involves a physical endurance element, such as a hike to the top of a mountain. She separates the boys and the girls for these initiations, to increase the comfort level of the group, and because the stories from the Bible and other sources which she tells each group are different.

Sometimes it isn't a rabbi who leads an initiation ritual for a bat mitzvah. Two sisters, Carrie and Laila Bernstein, both experienced an informal kind of initiation the day after their ceremonies in their backyard. Women relatives and friends gathered under a sheet for Carrie (her initiation was unplanned), and under a parachute for Laila (whose ceremony was a few years later). Carrie, and later Laila, stood in the middle of the circle, while the women gave them advice and tips.

Carrie says, "There was a lot of joking and good humor. Afterward they accepted me into the circle, and we danced around."

Laila remembers some of the advice. "They told me that bad experiences are part of the learning process and everything's a part of life. If something bad happens, it can help you grow. They also told me things like always keep a sewing kit in your purse, and how to fix a run in pantyhose (with clear nail polish)."

About this process of becoming a bat mitzvah, including the initiations, tutoring, and the *mitzvah* projects, Rabbi Gottlieb says, "By encouraging the building of our students' confidence and their own voice, by presenting them with a tremendous challenge, and by teaching them the ability to master the series of events in the Jewish coming of age, we strengthen their inner core. We help them develop the clarity of their own voice."

Recent studies, especially those published by Myra and David Sadker in *Failing at Fairness: How America's Schools Cheat Girls,* comment on how girls at this age are so often "invisible students, spectators to the educational process." Starting in about seventh grade, many girls begin to fall behind boys academically and lose self-confidence. Their teachers, often unintentionally, spend more time with the boys, and their textbooks devote only 2 percent of their space to women. One of the Sadkers' startling observations is that when classes at all age levels were asked to name twenty famous American women from history, excluding entertainers and athletes, many students could not name ten or even five.

The bat mitzvah ceremony and preparation come just at this crucial time in a girl's growing up that the Sadkers have studied. By its very nature, the bat mitzvah process can have an important role in building up a girl's self-esteem, her desire for achievement, her inner voice and direction.

Cheri Ellowitz Silver, the religious school director at Temple Israel of Hollywood, whose bat mitzvah ceremony was in 1965, says:

> *The bat mitzvah ceremony is incredibly well-timed as far as child development is concerned. The focus is on who I am and what I can achieve, and how I fit into the larger community. The student has a long-term goal, works towards it, achieves something, and feels good about it.*
>
> *My own bat mitzvah was a very positive experience for me. I found out I could sing, be in front of a group, and perform. I got a lot of pats on the back and later went on to get a B.A. in drama.*

• BAT MITZVAH •

My bat mitzvah was my first realization that I could be a performer, that I had talent.

In whatever way a girl prepares for her bat mitzvah ceremony, it will usually be a time of study, of the development of a close relationship with an adult who really cares about her, and a chance to explore her feelings about her religion, her family and herself. This preparation has the universal characteristic of coming-of-age ceremonies around the world and through the centuries—preparation for a coming challenge, a public challenge, an adult challenge.

This challenge is faced on the day of the ceremony, the day the bat mitzvah leads the congregation as a Jewish adult, and accepts the responsibilities of an adult before friends, family, and community.

WHAT'S GOING ON UP THERE?

The Ceremony

THE PLACE

For the bat mitzvah, the place where her ceremony is held is very familiar. She has prayed in the synagogue many times with her family and her community. But for those of you who are invited to a bat mitzvah ceremony and walk into a synagogue for the first time, there are many new and different objects around you, mostly in front of you.

Ritual Objects, or What *Is* That?

First, before you have even entered the sanctuary or chapel, you may have passed a rack with long fringed prayer shawls called *tallitot* (singular, *tallit*) hanging on it. These are worn around the neck and shoulders by men, and sometimes by women, depending on the custom of the particular synagogue. The history of this ritual garment goes back to ancient times, to the rectangular mantle or cloak that men wore then.

Often congregants will bring their own *tallitot* of varying sizes and designs. You may even see worshippers with large *tallitot* drape them over their head and shoulders during prayer to help them concentrate.

You will also pass by a container with head coverings, called *kippot* (singular, *kippah*) in Hebrew, *yarmulkes* in Yiddish. There may also be pieces of netting for married women to wear over their heads. Men, and sometimes women, wear the *kippot*. You can check the custom of the particular synagogue you are in by asking a member or an usher, or by looking around you and seeing what everyone else is doing.

While non-Jews, and some Jews do not wear a *tallit,* it is the custom in most synagogues for every male in the sanctuary to wear a *kippah* as a sign of respect for God.

As you sit down, the *bimah,* the pulpit from which the Torah is read, is in front of you. Traditionally it faces east, toward Jerusalem. This is where the people leading the service stand. The Ark, the wooden cabinet which holds the Torah scrolls, is usually at the back of the *bimah*. When the scrolls are taken out, you will notice they are decorated or dressed with fancy coverings, silver crowns, a silver breastplate, and a silver pointer that hangs downs in the front of the scroll.

During the reading of the Torah, the reader uses this pointer, the *yad,* to follow the words in the holy scroll. Readers are careful not to touch the parchment of the scroll with their fingers, because the skin's oils can cause damage to the scrolls over the years.

The congregation stands whenever the Ark is open and when the Torah is carried through the synagogue, as well as for certain prayers. Usually, the leader of the service lets you know when you stand or sit down.

Another object you may notice is a light suspended in front of and above the Ark. This is called a *ner tamid* or Eternal Light, and is kept burning always as a sign of God's presence. It also commemorates the Eternal Light that burned in the Tabernacle in Biblical times.

Often there will be a menorah—a branched candelabrum—or two on the *bimah,* to remind us of the ones in the Holy Temple that once stood in Jerusalem. These have seven branches. (You may be most familiar with the Hanukkah menorah, called a *hanukkiyah,* which has nine branches.)

The People

There will be many people on the *bimah* at different times during the service. Depending on the synagogue, there is usually a rabbi or a lay leader, a cantor who leads the singing, various people called up for honors, Torah readers and sometimes *gabbaim*—one or two people who stand on each side of the Torah reader to check and correct mistakes. Yes, even adults make mistakes when they read from the Torah!

The bat mitzvah will be on the *bimah* during the Torah reading part of the service, and sometimes before and after, depending on what else she will be leading.

Honors are often given to relatives and friends of the bat mitzvah and her family. Since the bat mitzvah ceremony is a community event, it is not only the family of the bat mitzvah who is honored. You will see other congregants honored as well.

These honors include *aliyot,* which entail chanting the blessings before and after the Torah reading, opening and closing the ark, holding the Torah, lifting and dressing the Torah after it is read, and leading a prayer or a reading.

The Words

The books you will need to follow the service are usually on your seat, in front of you, or near the door to the sanctuary on a table or bookstand. You'll need two books: the smaller one called a *siddur* or prayer book; and the larger book called a *Humash,* which has the Torah readings and *haftarot* in Hebrew and English, and English commentaries.

Hebrew is read from right to left, from the top of the page to the bottom. These books usually open from right to left, and page one is not where you would usually find it! If you do not read Hebrew, check to see if there is a special booklet available where the Hebrew has been transliterated. Many prayer books also contain transliterations for the important prayers that are sung aloud by the congregation.

Some More Tips for the Visitor

Just a few more things before the service begins. You may take a seat anywhere in the sanctuary, unless you are in an Orthodox synagogue where men and women sit in separate sections. Also, there may be a few congregants who like to sit in the same seat each time they attend services.

You may be surprised to see that not everyone arrives right when the service begins, the time the invitation stated. Particularly if this is a Conservative or Orthodox synagogue, and the service is hours long, people may arrive at different times. Usually everyone is there by the Torah reading, however. It is best to check with your host about the time you should arrive. You may want to ask your host ahead of time when the service ends as well. You might not be leaving the synagogue until 12:00 or 1:00 P.M., so be prepared!

Once the service begins, you may notice various unfamiliar movements people make while they are *davening,* praying. Certain bowing and bending movements are traditional and performed during prescribed parts of the service to show reverence for God. The swaying you may see is done according to personal taste. Some people find that swaying helps them concentrate during prayer.

You will also see some movement in and out of the sanctuary during the service for reasons of comfort. This is permissible, though not recommended during the Torah service and the rabbi's sermon. Just remember to put your prayer book on your seat and not on the floor, as a sign of respect, if you do leave the sanctuary.

Also, in some congregations you may notice people chatting during the service. It is best, however, to be attentive and respectful of the occasion.

With all the preliminaries over, you are now settled in your seat, watching the activity around you. There is an air of festivity, excitement, expectation. Like a holiday.

This is because Shabbat, the Sabbath, the time most frequently chosen for the bar or bat mizvah ceremony, is a holiday. From sundown

Friday evening until dark on Saturday (dark enough to see three stars in the sky), Jews all over the world celebrate the weekly holiday of the Sabbath. It is a time of rest, prayer, study, being with family and community. And of course, the bat mitzvah ceremony today adds special excitement.

IT'S FINALLY HERE: THE SERVICE

While you are finding your seat, the bat mitzvah is looking around the familiar sanctuary, seeing it fill up with school friends, with relatives, some from far away, with close family friends, and even business associates of her parents. There are also the faces she's used to seeing in this sanctuary, her Hebrew school classmates, her tutor, the rabbi, synagogue members who have wished her a good Shabbat every week.

If she did not know it before, she knows it now as she looks about her: Her day is really here. Finally here. This ceremony that she's worked for, prepared for, is about to begin. And all these people are here to witness and celebrate with her!

It all begins with a hush as the leader chants the opening prayers. The congregation joins in.

"How goodly are your tents, O Jacob . . ."

Suddenly, the bat mitzvah remembers what her Hebrew school teacher said about these introductory prayers, that they are "warm-ups" to get you ready for the rest of the service. They form a bridge between all those everyday thoughts you have on your mind and praying thoughts, thoughts of God and thanks, good deeds and peace, what you have done and what you could do and . . .

Do I need warm-ups today! a part of the bat mitzvah thinks, while the other part of her thinks, I'd like to get up there and get it over with.

It's comforting to have her mother and father sitting near her, her grandparents, and even her little sister. But it's hard sitting in the very first row. She turns slightly, looking for the encouraging smiles of friends behind her.

The singing in Hebrew around her has a happy tone, familiar, warm.

The heavens tell of the glory of God.

Day after day, night after night

The story is told.

There isn't a sound, not a word.

Yet the story echoes throughout the world.

The sun from its tent in the sky

Rises from the east and sweeps westward

Warming all the earth.

She feels all excited inside and nervous. Instead of the words of the Psalms running through her head, it's the words of the Torah and the haftarah going round and round, all mixed together.

Oh, I hope I don't get the Torah part mixed up with the haftarah part, she groans to herself. I hope it all comes out the way it's supposed to.

And, she thinks, my father's no help. She glances at him, his face almost shining with pride. Can you imagine him telling me everything's going to be okay, when I've heard all the stories about how he almost fainted at his own bar mitzvah! And Mom! She reaches to clasp my hands with hands as clammy as my own.

But she remembers her cousin Aaron's advice, and she remembers his bar mitzvah just a few months before. "No matter how much you practice, you're always going to make a mistake," he told her. "Don't worry about it. Even the adults make mistakes. Just take one word at a time."

She takes a deep breath. It's time to stand for the *barhu* prayer, the call to worship. The preliminaries are over. The morning service, *shaharit*, has begun. It's time to pay attention.

"Praise God, the Source of all blessings," the prayer leader intones in Hebrew.

Now she knows it's getting closer to the Torah reading, closer to her part.

She gets ready to sing the *Shema* with the whole congregation. This is a prayer she's known since she was a little girl, saying it with her parents every night before going to sleep. Her father calls it the listening prayer.

Listen, Israel, Adonai is our God, Adonai is One.

She takes the fringes of her *tallit* and wraps them around her fingers, the way her teacher in Hebrew school showed her. She rubs the silky strands, excited about wearing her *tallit* for the very first time in synagogue. It feels a little funny, different. Grown-up. But that's what today is all about, her mother says.

Now they're singing the middle part of the song that the Israelites sang after crossing the Red Sea, after leaving Egypt so long ago. She shivers, thinking of how ancient the prayers are. She shivers, too, because she knows the standing prayer, the *Amidah,* is next. It's getting closer to the time she will have to walk up the steps and face this big crowd of people.

In a way, she's glad for this time of quiet. Everyone standing together, praying to themselves. She whispers, "Please let me just get through it."

She reads all the blessings, all seven of them in the Sabbath *Amidah,* especially her favorite one, the very last. It's the one about peace. She always spends extra time on this one. Then she says a special thank you for bringing her family and friends together safely.

It's time for the cantor to repeat the *Amidah* out loud, in case there are some people who cannot say the prayers for themselves.

Okay, this is it. The rabbi is nodding in her direction. Ready or not. She takes her prayer book and walks, a little shakily, up the stairs. The smile on her face feels frozen. So do her arms and legs. She's up there singing, leading the whole congregation in the service for taking the Torah out of the Ark.

Somehow she sings the familiar words, feeling so grateful for all the months of practicing. Grateful, too, for the congregation that answers her and sings with her.

She's walking around the synagogue now with the Torah, a long parade of the rabbi, the cantor, and people being honored, with her in the lead. Her grandpa Moe is right behind her, and she sings the Hebrew in a loud clear voice.

Yours, O God, is the greatness and the power and the glory, the triumph and the majesty. For all in heaven and on earth is Yours.

She likes being in front of the procession. She smiles and nods at everyone. Now she can really see who's here. Grandma Anne gives her a squeeze as she passes by, and Cousin Aaron a wink. Everyone is beaming as they reach over to touch the Torah with their prayer book or *tallit,* and then kiss the part that touched the holy scroll.

She's happy, excited, hardly breathing, and thankful that everything works without her thinking about it. Her arms. Her legs. Her voice.

Slow down, she thinks. Her tutor always told her that, over and over again at her practices.

They're back on the *bimah*. The Torah is opened up on the reading platform, and the rabbi is calling all the people up for their honors.

She breathes a sigh of relief and sits down until she is called up for the hard part. She watches as her father and mother sing the blessings, her aunts and uncles, her grandparents and her Hebrew school teacher.

Then they call up Great-Grandpa Ben, who is ninety-one years old. Her grandfather and uncle have to help him up the stairs, and it takes a long time for him to reach the Torah. His voice cracks a lot, but sounds beautiful all the same. She fights back tears, remembering Pop Pop Ben's emergency surgery just last year.

Then it's her turn to chant the *maftir,* the very last section of the Torah reading for today. She walks up again. This time her smile feels real, because of Pop Pop Ben.

She sings the blessings, and then uses the pointer to touch the words in the Torah as she chants. She can't help but think, I'm doing what the rabbi does every week.

"You're great," the rabbi whispers to her when she finishes. "Just remember to go slowly."

The rabbi sits down. Everyone does. She's on the *bimah,* speaking all by herself. She reads her *Dvar Torah* explaining the haftarah. She tries to look up, but it makes her nervous to look out, especially at her friends who are making faces and thumbs-up signs. She looks at Cousin Aaron instead; she knows he remembers what it's like to be up here.

Before she realizes it, she's chanting the blessing before the haftarah from her little blue booklet. Then the haftarah. She wonders what her Christian friends think of all this. These strange ancient melodies that are nothing like the music they usually listen to. It's going fast, she thinks, as she begins the long blessing after the haftarah. She knows she's almost done, and tries not to race.

She's up to the last lines, thanking God for the Torah and the Sabbath. She closes her booklet with a loud snap and ducks, because she has seen her little sister passing out the "surprise" candy. Her tutor told her that it is an old tradition still observed in some synagogues—to wish her a sweet life.

All the people in the front rows stand up and throw. The candy comes pouring down on the *bimah,* but luckily Mom bought the soft kind, the wrapped-up jellies. Everyone is singing and clapping, and when the candy shower is over, all the little kids come running up to collect and eat the candy.

She remembers how Cousin Aaron hid a shield in the lectern to use for the candy throwing, and how everyone laughed when he pulled it out.

The worst is over, she thinks, relieved.

"You did beautifully," the rabbi says.

Then her parents come up for their speech.

Maybe the worst isn't over, she thinks, hoping they won't embarrass her and talk about what she was like as a baby or something.

She feels frozen again, but warm inside, watching the way her parents are smiling at her. Their words go by so fast. It's hard to pay attention in front of all these people. She hears them say "proud" and "wish for" and "years of study" and "good deeds." She cringes. Oh, no. Now they're talking about how well she does in school and her extracurricular activities. Please. Don't let them talk about boys.

Then the president of the synagogue comes up, and talks about her, too, and gives her a present. It's a *Kiddush* cup with her name on it and the date of her bat mitzvah. "To use when you make the blessing over the wine every Sabbath, and the holidays, too," she says.

They walk in another procession, getting ready to return the Torah to the ark. Her legs and arms don't feel stiff anymore. It's almost over and she has gotten through it. She's grinning, a real grin, not a plastered one.

This time, as they go around the synagogue, she sees some people she didn't see before. She feels overwhelmed by all the people who have come. And some from so far.

She goes back to the front row while the rabbi gives the sermon. Hands are reaching out to shake hers as she goes by. Voices say, "*Yeeshar kohaykh*. May you grow in strength."

Her father smiles and her mother whispers, "Great!" as she takes her place. Her friends tap her on the shoulder so she'll turn around.

The rabbi talks about the Torah reading and what it means for us

95

today, then calls her up for a special blessing. The rabbi's hands feel warm and loving on her head.

The service lasts just a little longer. Good thing, too, the bat mitzvah thinks, because suddenly she feels hungry. Starving! She remembers how she could hardly eat any breakfast. Breakfast! That seems ages ago. Another world. Another time and place.

The cantor sings, and this time, during the second standing prayer, she says a big silent thank you. She made it! No major mistakes! No fainting. No giggling. No losing her place. Thank You, thank You, thank You.

The words to her favorite song in the whole service fill the sanctuary. The peace song. They repeat the tune over and over. *Oseh Shalom.* Please, God, make peace in the world.

They say the very last prayers, including the *Kaddish,* the mourner's prayer, the one that doesn't even talk about death at all, but about the glory of God's creation.

She hears the rabbi say, "Please join us in the social hall for a *Kiddush* honoring the bat mitzvah. Kindly wait before you drink or eat for the proper blessings."

Everyone lets her pass so she can greet each person at the door. She's so happy. She did it! It wasn't easy. All those months of practice for such a short time. But it was worth it. She would do it again!

BNOT MITZVAH SPEAK

Not every single bat mitzvah ceremony has the exact order or parts of the service described above. However, this is one typical framework, with each synagogue and rabbi adding their specific style. This one is a composite Saturday morning bat mitzvah ceremony taken from several girls' interviews.

Some ceremonies may not be on a Saturday morning at all. They may be held another time the Torah is read, such as on a Monday or a Thursday morning, a Saturday afternoon, *Rosh Hodesh,* or a holiday. If the family chooses a Saturday afternoon, the bat mitzvah often leads a ritual called *havdallah,* which marks the end of the Sabbath, in addition to reading from the Torah. Also, the ceremony is sometimes held on a day when the Torah is not read, such as a Sunday.

Here are some comments from teens about their experiences after their big day.

"I'd do it again," says Ayana Morse. "I was nervous for months and weeks before. When the event came, I was totally calm and happy. I wanted the service to be over and breathed a huge sigh of relief when it was.

"I felt like I had accomplished something big in my life.

"Reading the Torah was a very special part. It was something I'd never done before in front of people. It was amazing to know I could do it. It's a hard thing to make music out of a bunch of words smooshed together on the page.

"If I had a chance to do it again, I definitely would. Except for the times when my dear little sister, Leah, was jealous of me.

"It began about a month before, when everyone had the invitations and I started getting presents. Leah dropped hints like, 'How come no one's sending me these gifts?' or 'You're getting all the attention.' She kept on getting more and more jealous as I got more and more presents, especially when the money came.

"I actually gave her a present on my bat mitzvah—earrings. It

97

didn't help much. It kept her quiet for a little bit. I really did go out of my way to be nice to her.

"When we were walking to synagogue on the day of my bat mitzvah, my sister decided she wasn't going to help pass out the candy after I did the haftarah. She was steaming mad. She threatened she wouldn't lead *Adon Olam,* the song at the end, either. I was heartbroken. Then, in the end, my Dad convinced her to do both.

"Just make sure someone gives something to the younger kid, too."

Unlike Ayana, Suzette Krausen has a younger brother who actually behaved much better than she expected during her big day. She, too, felt it was very special to be able to read from the Torah. Suzette says, "The bat mitzvah ceremony brings you one step closer to God. Now I'm able to read from the Torah, God's words. Wearing a *tallit* feels special, especially one my Pop Pop gave me."

A lot of Suzette's non-Jewish friends came to her service. She discovered that they loved the singing. "They listen to rhythm and blues, and really liked the cantor's voice."

Rachel Diamond invited her whole class from school to her bat mitzvah ceremony. Most of the students were not Jewish, and they all came. "They thought it was pretty neat," she says.

"One of the special moments was when I came down from the *bimah,*" she continues. "I had to go to the door of the sanctuary and shake hands with everyone. There were all these people I hadn't seen in years. It felt like a family reunion. Everybody was congratulating me, saying I did great. I was relieved and proud all together.

"I did have a couple of minutes of real nervousness, though. When I actually had to go to the *bimah,* I knew this was *it.* I started crying and was trying to control it, trying to keep a calm face. My dad handed me a tissue. I was so scared that I was going to mess up. When I started to sing, my voice was shaky. But as I got into it, I wasn't nervous anymore."

Ariela Perlmutter had a moment of confusion during her service that made her nervous, but she handled it well. Her bat mitzvah ceremony was in June. She says, "It was really hot up there on the *bimah*. Right after I read the haftarah, I must have been relieved and hot, too, and I blew my bangs up off my forehead. But I didn't realize I had done this.

"Everyone laughed at this gesture. They must have thought it was cute or something. I didn't know why they were laughing, because I didn't know I had done anything. I kept going and tried to think of what I'd messed up on."

Elaina Deutsch is used to being in front of people because she acts in plays at school. Still, she says, "I was afraid I was going to mess up. But it turned out to be fine. And actually I did more than the rabbi did."

Elaina goes on to say, "I think my becoming a bat mitzvah made me think more about my religion. I like services more now and understand them better. I didn't like to go when I was younger. I felt like I was forced to go. But it's different now."

Shoshana Bannett says she didn't feel nervous about the parts of the service she'd gone over a lot. "The Friday before the ceremony, I practiced in the sanctuary and looked at my portion in the actual Torah scroll I would be reading from. That helped a lot. We also took pictures of me reading from the Torah that Friday afternoon, since we wouldn't be allowed to take photos at my actual ceremony."

Her advice is, "Don't try to get away with the least possible amount of work. Don't try and skimp on it. You'll get more out of becoming a bat mitzvah if you do as much as you can."

Alison Rodin describes how putting on her prayer shawl, her *tallit,* on the day of her bat mitzvah ceremony signified something important to her. "It was a very special moment. I knew there was no turning back. I knew I wasn't just practicing anymore. This was real. Wearing the *tallit* reminded me that God was there."

Carrie Bernstein describes her experience like this: "At first, the bat mitzvah was my parents' idea. I disliked studying for my bat mitzvah, loathed it. It was hard work because I didn't want to do it. Memorization is difficult for me. I wasn't sure if it would be a positive or negative experience. I was worried that I would feel like an imposter on the *bimah.*

"But when I was on the *bimah,* it was an amazing experience. I felt close to God for the first time in my life. Before this, I had felt that I didn't have a place in the synagogue. I got lost during the service. But during my bat mitzvah, I felt connected.

"That experience changed my feeling toward the service. When I was singing the haftarah, I felt warmth, partially a sense of being tied into tradition. I was helping the Jewish tradition perpetuate. I felt the blessings had meaning. I felt guilty that I hadn't believed what I was saying before I was up there. I had been afraid I would feel like my speech was a lie. It didn't feel meaningful until I was up there. I still feel connected when I go to synagogue now. The warm feeling is still there.

"Now I look back fondly at the preparation and am proud, like I've accomplished something. It was very empowering. I have the sense that I could do it again."

Carrie's sister, Laila, says about her bat mitzvah ceremony: "Perfection isn't it. Recovering from mistakes is what's important. I felt really supported at my ceremony. When you have a big tournament, there's an opposing team who doesn't want you to do well. But here, everyone is rooting for you.

"I had a part in the Friday night service and that helped. I got used to being up there, and it was less formal than Saturday morning.

"After my bat mitzvah, I realized that I knew more than I thought I did. It gave me a sense of being able to participate when it's not my bat mitzvah. The Jewish aspects of my life came together, and I have a very positive feeling of being Jewish now.

"At my synagogue, we have to write a prayer besides a speech. My prayer is about peace and justice. Writing the speech and the prayer made me feel closer to God. When I did them in the synagogue, I felt there was a presence there helping me along. It felt like the right place to do this—a sacred place.

"I find I go to services more now because of the bat mitzvah, and feel closer to God. The silent prayer helps me think—of problems in my life and what to pray for. It helps me decide and make priorities. Synagogue feels like a protected place to think and pray."

Katya Schapiro had no formal Hebrew education until sixth grade. She says, "I decided to find out whether I wanted a bat mitzvah or not. My friends who went to Hebrew school griped about it, but then I caught onto the fact that I might be missing something. We hired a tutor who taught me to read Hebrew, taught me about prayers, Jewish concepts—a basic introduction to Judaism. She was able to answer my questions, too.

101

"The idea of having a bat mitzvah got me much more interested in Judaism. But my interest ended up being for its own sake, not just for a bat mitzvah. I gained a community—the most important thing for me at the temple. And all the adults there love me because I drew my family closer to Judaism."

For Katya, one of the more meaningful aspects of her bat mitzvah was hearing what people said about her at her ceremony. "I had been going to other ceremonies and hearing what people said to the bar or bat mitzvah—their parents, the rabbi, the synagogue president. I liked hearing what my parents said, what they came up with after thirteen years of knowing me.

"After my bat mitzvah, my *havurah* presented me with a book. Each member wrote something, and put drawings or photographs or something that represented how they felt about me in the book. They also wrote messages for me. A cousin of mine liked the book so much that my mother made one for her when she became a bat mitzvah."

Shoshana Zonderman put together a similar book for her daughter Ariela. Before the bat mitzvah, she gave photo album pages to relatives and friends who filled them with quotes, photographs, and collages to wish Ariela well. She also put out blank paper at the celebration for guests to write something to the bat mitzvah. Afterward, she collected these loose pages into a "blessing book" as a keepsake for Ariela.

Elizabeth Goldman's family is a member of an Orthodox synagogue. She also goes with her mother to a women's service once a month at a different synagogue. She chose to have her ceremony at the women's service, and then later walk to her family's synagogue and give a *Dvar Torah,* a talk about the Torah portion, there. In this way, the men who couldn't come to the women's service (remember, only nine men are allowed behind the *mehitzah*) could hear her speech in the afternoon.

She says, "At my regular synagogue, most girls have a Sunday brunch or a *Kiddush* on Saturday and give a *Dvar Torah.* But we wanted to do more. If I just did a *Dvar Torah,* I wouldn't get the feeling that I was an adult. That was my dream—to do what everybody in the service did. It gave me confidence that I could do all this and other things, not just in Judaism. I had a solo in graduation and I was a little more confident because of my bat mitzvah."

A special moment for Elizabeth came after she finished chanting. "At the women's service, there is no *bimah.* The Torah is placed on a table. When I finished chanting, everyone came up and hugged me. They danced around me and the Torah and sang *mazal tov v'simin tov*—the congratulations song. It made me feel good that so many people cared.

"My bat mitzvah, the fact that I became a Jewish woman, made me think more seriously about what I do. It made me realize that I have to start paying attention. I have to take charge and do the right thing. Now is when it's really important."

Elizabeth didn't learn her *maftir* and haftarah from a casette tape. She advises, "Don't memorize it from a tape. If you learn the *trop* instead of just memorizing, then you can do it again. Now I have real skills I can use forever."

Dena Landowne Bailey, the oldest of three daughters, was the first in her family to become bat mitzvah, in June of 1984. Also from an

Orthodox family, she chose to have a very informal ceremony in her home, on a Sunday, where she gave a talk on a topic she had studied with her mother. Because of the size of her house and the number of people she wanted to invite, Dena ended up having three separate seatings of guests and giving her talk more than once!

Dena says, "My bat mitzvah ceremony was just another step in my Jewish life. What made me really feel my coming of age were the changes in my obligations as an adult Jewish woman, like fasting on all the fast days, and not being able to go into the men's section of the synagogue anymore."

Her mother-in-law, Sheila Stein Bailey, remembers her bat mitzvah ceremony in 1958. Her whole class at an Orthodox Jewish girls' school in Baltimore celebrated a group bat mitzvah ceremony with a dinner and the presentation of a program. She says the emphasis then wasn't on women learning. They learned Bible and laws and customs and Jewish history in their all-girl classes, but not everything that boys learned. She says that now there is an awakening—thousands of women are learning Talmud in Israel and in the United States, subjects in Judaism that girls didn't study when she was young.

Two of the girls I talked to experienced specific problems that caused them to worry before and during their ceremonies. Both had parents who had separated and were going through a divorce.

One says, "I was really worried my parents would actually have a fight right there during the service. But they didn't. They even sat on the same row in front, one on each side of my brother and me."

The other says, "The hardest thing was having my parents separated. Taking pictures was hard. And who's going to pay for what? Then there's what do you put at the bottom of the invitation? We solved that problem by having the invitation come from me, with my name at the bottom instead of my parents."

It can be helpful if a girl in this situation has someone outside the family she can express her concerns to. An adult she trusts and feels comfortable with could be a relative, a counselor, the rabbi, or her tutor. The important thing was that, for both these girls, their day was one they'll remember all their lives, as it is for each and every girl who becomes a bat mitzvah.

EMPTY CHAIRS AND MOUNTAIN FORTRESSES: UNUSUAL CEREMONIES AND PLACES

Each bat mitzvah ceremony is unique and special and different, whether it is held in a synagogue sanctuary, someone's living room, or outdoors under the stars.

Just to give you some idea of the range of possibilities, here are some ceremonies that have been held in unusual places, under circumstances that are worth knowing about.

Some girls and their families go to Israel to have the ceremony, often to Masada. Masada was an isolated mountain fortress on the edge of the Judean Desert, of great importance in the war with the Romans. It was the last holdout, and was not conquered until three years after Jerusalem, in 73 c.e. It has become a place of pilgrimage, and a symbol of courage and determination.

In 1983, Malia Aharoni of Honolulu, Hawaii, chose a different site in Israel for her bat mitzvah cermony—one that had never been used for this kind of ceremony before—the tomb of the Matriarch Rachel outside Bethlehem.

─────── • What's Going On Up There? • ───────

Stacey and Jana Kofman, sixteen-year-old twin sisters, toured Israel for six weeks in 1984. They were deeply inspired by their trip, especially a Friday night service at the Western Wall, a section of the supporting wall of the Holy Temple which survived destruction over the centuries and has become a sacred place for many Jews. On their return home, they decided to study for a bat mitzvah ceremony and asked their mother, Lynn Miller, to join them.

They had to start at the very beginning with the Hebrew alphabet. Two years later, the three shared a bat mitzvah ceremony at their synagogue in San Francisco. "I only wish my parents were alive to see this," said their mother afterward.

In 1990, Yiling Livia Chen-Josephson became the first girl in China's history to have a bat mitzvah ceremony there.

Persian Jews had come to China as early as the eighth century as traders along the famed Silk Road. Some settled in Kaifeng and married Chinese women, but still observed traditional Jewish customs into the nineteenth century. Their synagogue fell into ruin in the 1850s, following the last rabbi's death.

"I hope the fact that I had my bat mitzvah ceremony in Kaifeng shows how far females have progressed," Yiling told her guests.

Yiling, whose mother is Chinese, and whose father is a Jewish American, converted to Judaism as a child. She says she's "conscious of being Jewish, Chinese, and American all at once."

To help her with her service in Kaifeng, a rabbi, cantor, Torah scroll, and of course family and guests, were flown in from New York, where Yiling lives.

Her father says he wanted to have the ceremony in China to honor both sides of his daughter's heritage. He was inspired by a newspaper

107

article about an American boy who held his bar mitzvah ceremony in Krakow, Poland, to honor the memory of his Polish relatives who were killed during the Holocaust.

At her ceremony in New York, Alisa Jancu had an empty chair placed on the *bimah* with a sign on it that read DINA ALTMAN. Dina was Alisa's bat mitzvah "twin." Dina's family were *refuseniks* in the Soviet Union. They had asked to leave the Soviet Union in 1976 to join their relatives in Israel, but their application had been refused. And Dina, like many Soviet Jewish thirteen-year-olds of the time, could not have a coming-of-age ceremony.

Alisa says, "Since my ceremony, I had dreamed of meeting Dina when she got out of the Soviet Union, but I never thought I would see her before she gained her freedom."

In 1987, a year after her bat mitzvah ceremony, Alisa and her mother traveled to Tashkent, in the central Asian part of what was then the Soviet Union, and managed to find the Altmans' apartment.

"I had brought presents for them," Alisa says, "among which was a gold *hai* pin for Dina [*hai* means life]. She and her parents did not know what it was. The grandmother, who still remembered her Jewish heritage, explained the meaning to them. This depressing scene showed me that for some families, the Soviet policy of not permitting Jewish education was succeeding."

Dina and Alisa embraced like sisters when it was time for the Jancus to go. For Alisa, Dina Altman was no longer just a name on a sign on an empty chair at her bat mitzvah ceremony.

Another girl who decided to share her ceremony is Alison Geare. Her "twin" was Amy Joyce Glass, a young woman of nineteen who has Down's syndrome, a chromosomal disorder that causes limited intellectual abilities and distinctive physical characteristics. Amy received tutoring, and although she cannot read, she was able to learn and recite the *Shema* at the ceremony.

Alison says, "I feel that people who have special needs should have a chance to participate in something like this."

So much has happened since 1922 and the first bat mitzvah ceremony! Probably there will be many more changes in the years ahead of us, as girls and women think about what a Jewish girl's coming-of-age ceremony can be.

"WHAT CHOCOLATE-COVERED STRAWBERRIES?"

Celebrating

The afterward part of the bat mitzvah's day, the celebration, is very important to the girls who've done all this work and "gotten through it alive," as Josee says.

"When you're thirteen, life is hard enough," Shoshana says. "You're changing. Friends are changing. There's all that bickering. But none of this goes on at the party. It's a nice break. For one night you can have fun. You look great. The work's over. You don't get too many chances to throw a party with friends and relatives like that."

The celebrating begins with the *Kiddush* held in the synagogue right after the service. Everyone gathers around, sings the blessings over wine and bread, eats, and congratulates the bat mitzvah and her family.

Many *bnot mitzvah* have an additional party in the afternoon or evening. These vary tremendously, but usually include a meal and sometimes entertainment.

The history of the coming-of-age party goes back hundreds of years. The party was not just a custom, but a religious obligation. A Jewish code of law of the 1500s, called the *Shulhan Arukh,* stated that it was the father's religious obligation to offer a festive meal in honor of his son's becoming a bar mitzvah, just as he would do later when the son married.

This celebration usually took the form of a meal in the family's home after the ceremony. The bar mitzvah often gave a religious talk during the meal.

THE REAL THEME

As old as the bar mitzvah party is, just as old is the worry by Jewish community leaders over the extravagance of these parties. They worried that fancy feasts would overpower the religious importance of the coming-of-age ceremony.

Among the laws passed to control the celebration was one in 1595 in Poland which placed a communal tax on bar mitzvah feasts so they would not become excessive displays of wealth. Also in Poland, in 1659 a decree stated that no more than ten strangers could be invited to a bar mitzvah feast, and one of them must be a poor man.

Today we do not have such laws, but some Jewish leaders are still concerned about the excesses of the parties. Comments range from, "I've seen every theme at bar and bat mitzvah celebrations except human sacrifice" to, "What's wrong with the real theme of bat and bar mitzvah: Jewish commitment?"

In a magazine article, Rabbi Lawrence Kushner of Sudbury, Massachusetts, says, "All the circumstances that once prevailed at weddings now prevail at bar/bat mitzvah time. The desire for a major celebration is very strong and deeply rooted. We can't stop people from feeling this way; we just have to find a way to channel the feelings constructively."

In the same article, Rabbi Jeffrey Salkin of Rockville Centre, New York, says, "It's not what you spend—it's what you give. [An expensive] bar mitzvah that includes a substantial donation to a charitable organization is morally and Jewishly preferable to a more modest affair where no *tzedakah* is given."

A Los Angeles–based organization called Mazon, A Jewish Response to Hunger (*mazon* is the Hebrew word for "food"), provides an avenue for families to give part of the cost of their celebration to *tzedakah*. It is a direct response to community feeling about putting Jewish ethics back into family celebrations. Families voluntarily add 3 percent to the cost of their celebrations—a bar or bat mitzvah, a wedding, a birthday or anniversary, any joyous occasion—and send this amount to Mazon to help defeat hunger at home and around the world.

DJs AND SOFTBALL GAMES

Whatever the controversy over the elaborateness of the party, there is no question that a bat mitzvah deserves and looks forward to a celebration after her ceremony.

The parties are as individual as the bat mitzvah and her family, the customs of her local synagogue and her community—and reflect the values of both. There are outdoor lunches under a big tent. DJs run the circuit of some Jewish communities offering limbo contests and the latest in popular music. There are vegetarian potlucks in the park and luncheons at home cooked by loving relatives and friends.

One family had the party in the hall of dinosaurs of a city museum of natural history. An athletically oriented bat mitzvah reserved a picnic area in a public park and had a potluck dinner followed by baseball games for her celebration. And for Talya Husband-Hankin's celebration, her family made a party at the beach. Talya helped choose the food and make the decorations. All the food was homemade; some dishes they prepared themselves and some were brought by guests, potluck style.

Themes are sometimes chosen for the party. Other than human sacrifice, they include everything from luaus, sports, and Israel, to favorite rock groups. Usually the bat mitzvah is involved in the actual planning and decision making of the party. This enables her to feel it is really her celebration.

Josee says, "I made sure all of my food was vegetarian because I'm vegetarian, and I believe you shouldn't eat meat. It made the food kosher, too."

Suzette helped choose the DJ for her party. She says, "I'd been to two other parties Big Al did. I wanted him. I talked to him a lot about all sorts of things—about how I was nervous, how my grandmother, who'd been sick, was going to come. He took a real interest in me."

Katya says, "My party wasn't at a fancy place. We looked all around and decided we didn't have to be stuffy. It was reasonable, so we had enough money to hire a band.

"This was the first time I ever enjoyed a large party. The first time I

was the center of attention without guilt. I had earned it. People were proud of me. The ceremony was over and I could relax. I didn't have to worry about something else. I didn't have to worry about people criticizing me, because it was my party and I'd done something important for me and my family."

Elaina helped write a speech for a candle ceremony at her party where each relative or friend named came up to light a candle on her bat mitzvah cake. She says, "I was recognizing other people and wasn't just thinking of myself. The people we called up meant a lot to me."

And several of the girls' parties did have Jewish content. Shoshana Bannett had musicians who played Israeli music and someone who taught Israeli dancing, along with a buffet offering typical Israeli food

such as falafel. Both Ariela and Katya had klezmer bands that played Yiddish folk tunes. Klezmer bands originated in Eastern Europe, where musicians would go from town to town entertaining at joyous occasions. They played a variety of instruments including trumpet, flute, clarinet, violin, cello, bass, and drum.

Shira Rockowitz of New Rochelle, New York, says, "We've had a lot of the same disco parties over and over again. I wanted to do something Jewish." On the day following her bat mitzvah service and *Kiddush,* her friends, close relatives, and Shira boarded a bus for Manhattan. After eating a typical Lower East Side snack of pickles and black bread with raisins, the group went to the Eldridge Street Synagogue, the first synagogue built by Eastern European immigrants in New York, in 1887, to help in its revival. They sang as they polished brass, and dusted and swept their way around the long-abandoned main sanctuary. Afterward they went to a local restaurant for one last taste of the Lower East Side. One of the guests commented, "That was really special. When I'm older I can tell my kids I helped to restore this synagogue."

The party, no matter what kind, is usually a great whirlwind of people, activity, and feelings for the bat mitzvah, and can also have its own set of difficulties.

Rachel says, "There were so many people around saying 'hi' at the party, I almost didn't get to eat anything. One of my friends said, 'Oh, those chocolate-covered strawberries were so great!' I said, 'What chocolate-covered strawberries?' "

Ayana's comment was, "I tried to be in so many places at once and make everyone happy."

And looking back on her party, Ariela has this to say: "I regret leaving with my school friends. It was hot and we played over at the pool [of the hotel] instead of staying under the tent with the other guests. When my family and I started talking about the party afterward, especially when all the pictures came back, I realized I didn't remember all the stuff that had gone on and who was there."

Shoshana talks about a friend whose bat mitzvah day was in March of 1993, on the weekend of a giant snowstorm. "My friend cried herself to sleep the night before. But almost everyone still came. The caterers and the band came, and the people. She had a much better day than she expected."

Another bat mitzvah had the feuding-relatives problem. She says, "The trouble with my great-aunts and my grandmother came about

116

when they had to split up things in my great-grandmother's house after she died. That caused trouble with the seating arrangement at the party. We couldn't put them all at the same table. So we put my grandparents with friends, and the great-aunts together. In the end, it worked out okay."

Another girl, whose parents are divorced, solved the problem of seating arrangements at the party by not having any. She just put name cards on her friends' tables and let the adults choose their own places.

This same girl says, "My mother wanted to have a Sabbath feeling to the party, and we didn't have a lot of money, so we didn't hire a DJ or a band. But it was chaos after the meal.

"The luncheon place had an upstairs and a downstairs. The little kids ran up and down the stairs, while the kids my age went in and out the windows. The woman in charge kept telling me to watch the kids, big and little. Looking back on it, we should have hired baby-sitters for the younger kids, and a mime or some kind of entertainment for the older ones. And maybe had it all in one big room."

But whatever difficulties came up, the girls agreed that the big day was worth it all.

Ayana says, "I'd do anything for a good party!"

And Rachel says, "It was fun to be the center of attention for a weekend from my parents and other people, to be in the middle of things. It was really 'my day.'"

"Everyone is there for you and listening to you," Ariela adds.

"It was fun," Josee says. "My family made such a big fuss over me. After everybody left, I felt sorry it was over."

IS IT REALLY ALL OVER?
Afterward

וּדְבוֹרָה אִשָּׁה נְבִיאָה אֵשֶׁת לַפִּידוֹת הִיא שֹׁפְטָה אֶת־יִשְׂרָאֵל
בָּעֵת הַהִיא: וְהִיא יוֹשֶׁבֶת תַּחַת־תֹּמֶר דְּבוֹרָה בֵּין הָרָמָה וּבֵין
בֵּית־אֵל בְּהַר אֶפְרָיִם וַיַּעֲלוּ אֵלֶיהָ בְּנֵי יִשְׂרָאֵל לַמִּשְׁפָּט:
וַתִּשְׁלַח וַתִּקְרָא לְבָרָק בֶּן־אֲבִינֹעַם מִקֶּדֶשׁ נַפְתָּלִי וַתֹּאמֶר

—*Judges 4:4-6*

Many girls besides Josee describe a letdown feeling after it's all over. Elaina says, "I'd been studying for so long and it was over in one day. That seemed strange."

Shoshana felt that way, too. "A week later, when I went to someone else's bat mitzvah, I felt a little jealous. I had prepared and worked so hard. I need more turns, I thought, than only one day."

She says one thing that was helpful was having a brunch at their house the next day, on Sunday morning. "Everyone around here does that. It lengthens the whole thing. When you're so hyped up and then there's nothing, that's rough. The brunch was a quieter time. People came by word of mouth, not by a written invitation. There were bagels and leftovers from the party. Nothing fancy. Then it's not all over quite so fast."

But *is* it all over after the big day? What happens in the life of the bat mitzvah after a milestone event like this one, where the community nity recognizes that this girl has now come of age as far as ritual maturity and commitment?

NOW I AM A JEWISH ADULT

Several girls had stories about how they were now an "adult" in the Jewish world. Josee says, "I was more respected in my family and felt more a part of my community. A few years ago, in my *havurah,* there was an older boy who had just become a bar mitzvah. The adults were playing a game. They said, 'Jacob, you can come in because you are a Jewish adult.' I felt left out. Now I can say I am a Jewish adult. I feel more a part of things."

Ariela tells how she was eating ice cream in the living room. Her mother said, "You're not supposed to eat in here." Ariela answered, "Why not? You are." Her mother said, "I'm an adult." Ariela used her recent coming of age for leverage and said, "Well, I'm an adult, too." She got to eat her ice cream in the living room.

Ayana says that becoming a bat mitzvah "made me feel that now I'm an adult in Judaism and my opinion counts more than it did before."

FINDING A NICHE

Shoshana, who was sixteen and a half at the time of her interview, talks about how she had expectations of her Jewish community that weren't met after she became a bat mitzvah. "I was so excited. I felt so Jewish, such a part of my heritage. It was hard to find a niche after that. They [the Jewish community, the synagogue] spend so much time with you. And then they don't invest much in you.

"The cantor who had trained me left after my ceremony. That connection was gone. I went to the Hebrew High School program for a while, but the kids my age stopped going, one by one. I tried a youth group and other things, but had a hard time finding anything to connect with Jewishly after I became a bat mitzvah. I really thought I would feel more integral to the Jewish community. It just didn't meet my expectations.

"But now they're starting a group for post–*bnai mitzvah* students at my synagogue. They'll cover Judaism as seen through Christian eyes, have clergy and Catholic teenagers come, and have other topics about Judaism that kids my age are interested in. I'm glad about this."

Her advice is, "Be patient. Just try to remember the feeling you had during the ceremony and you'll feel it again. It may take a while. Just don't expect everything to change after you become a bat mitzvah."

Many people working with *bnai mitzvah* students are concerned for *bnai mitzvah* to be counted as part of the community much more than they are. They can be asked to read Torah on the anniversary of their ceremonies, and other times if they can learn new portions. There could be Sabbath services which the teens lead.

Hanna Tiferet Siegel says, "The democratization of Judaism should not be just within the adult community, but among the *bnai mitzvah* as well. We need to affirm that they are now counted as part of the community. We don't make enough of that."

And Martha Ackelsberg says, "I wonder if we shouldn't be doing more to make an opportunity to think about bat mitzvah, to use that time to reflect on women's position in Judaism, because we've still got a long way to go. What does the bat mitzvah want from Judaism, from her community? What does she want to give?

"The bat mitzvah is now coming into full membership in the Jewish community? What is her version of the Judaism she would like to be a part of?"

BEING PART OF A COMMUNITY

Some *bnot mitzvah* have found their own ways to fit into and contribute to their Jewish communities. Suzette volunteers in the Sunday school of her synagogue with the fifth-grade class and helps the teacher while her mother teaches one of the other classes.

Another teen cares for a group of preschool children at her synagogue, while their parents teach in the Hebrew school. Some travel and bring their experiences and enthusiasms back to their communities. One trip that has a special impact on teens is a tour of concentration camp sites in Eastern Europe followed by Israel and the Holocaust Memorial there.

Other teens are involved in classes for those who have come of age, continuing their Jewish studies both formally and informally; join youth groups; work in synagogue offices; lead parts of synagogue services; are counselors in Jewish summer camps; or volunteer in social action programs of their synagogues. Social action projects range from helping the homeless and serving food in soup kitchens to bringing refugees over from war-torn countries such as Bosnia. The community helps the refugees settle in local towns and cities by finding apartments, furniture, clothing, and jobs for the newcomers.

Carrie Bernstein and her friends formed a group called Students

Organized to Advocate Peace. After months of selling raffle tickets, washing cars, selling T-shirts, raking leaves, and sponsoring a contra dance and bake sale, these girls raised about three thousand dollars.

With this money, they paid the plane fares and expenses for two girls, refugees from the Croatian city of Zagreb, to come to Amherst, Massachusetts, in February 1994. The Croatian girls stayed with host American families, attended the local high school, and had a respite from the war going on in their homeland.

Carrie says, "We wanted to educate people here about what it's like to live in a society similar to the United States in terms of privilege and wealth, and then to have all that taken away. We researched the problem and found something we could do that would touch lives. My bat mitzvah helped me see how important community is to a group of people, especially to an oppressed group. Jews were an oppressed group in the Holocaust, and Bosnia is now."

Many *bnai mitzvah* express a strong desire to act to improve their world. They're worried about what kind of world they're inheriting and growing up into. Rabbi Sue Elwell says, "This ceremony marks the bat mitzvah's growth and prepares her for future learning and responsibility to the community, both the synagogue community and the larger community. Bat mitzvah can give a girl a sense of who she is in relation to the world, to the Jewish people, and who she is in the context of her family. Also, becoming a bat mitzvah gives a young girl a new sense of responsibility to herself."

The *bnot mitzvah* of today—these young women of twelve and thirteen—are strong and powerful individuals with a lot to say about themselves, their experiences, and their communities. And the bat mitzvah ceremony is not an isolated event in their lives or in their communities. The girls and their ceremonies are part of an ongoing search for individual spiritual fulfillment and for connection with and responsibility to a community. All the energy and effort that is currently going into bat mitzvah preparation and ceremony is part of what our generation is writing in its own chapter of Jewish women's history.

GLOSSARY

Aliyah (ah-lee-YAH or ah-LEE-yah) is the honor of being called up to say the blessings before and after the Torah portion is read. Plural: **aliyot** (ah-lee-YOAT)

B.C.E. stands for Before the Common Era, and is used by Jews instead of B.C. to mark the years before the year one in the standard modern numbering. (C.E. stands for Common Era and is used instead of A.D.)

Bar Mitzvah (bar mitz-VAH or bar MITZ-vah) means "one who has the obligation of fulfilling commandments." At thirteen years and one day, a boy becomes responsible for following the rules of adult Jewish life. Plural: **bnai mitzvah**.

Bat Mitzvah (baht mitz-VAH or baht MITZ-vah) means "one who has the obligation of fulfilling commandments." At twelve years and one day, a girl becomes responsible for following the rules of adult Jewish life. Plural: **bnot mitzvah**.

Bimah (bee-MAH or BEE-mah) is the raised platform in most synagogues from which the Torah scroll is read.

Cantor (CAN-ter) is the person who leads the singing parts of the synagogue service.

Conservative Judaism (kun-SERV-uh-tiv) is a movement that opposes extreme changes in traditional observances, but permits some modifications in response to changes in the life and times of the Jewish people.

Converso (cone-VER-so) refers to the non-Christians who converted to Christianity under the force of the Spanish Inquisition beginning in the late fifteenth century. Jews or Muslims who refused to convert were expelled from Spain and Portugal. Another term for the convert (or New Christian), which in the past has had a derogatory connotation, is **Marrano**. Plural: **conversos**.

Dvar Torah (duh-VAR toe-RAH or duh-VAR TOE-ruh) is a talk based on the weekly Torah reading.

Gabbai (GOB-eye) is the person who stands near the Torah reader and carefully follows the reading from a printed text. It is the gabbai's duty to correct the Torah reader if he or she makes a mistake. Plural: **gabbaim** (gob-by-YEEM or gob-BY-im)

Haftarah (hahf-tah-RAH or hahf-TOE-rah) is a selection from the Prophets which is read after the weekly Torah portion. It means "concluding portion." Plural: **haftarot** (haf-tar-OAT)

Hasidism (ha-SEED-ism) is a movement founded by Israel ben Eliezer, known as the Baal Shem Tov, in the late 1700s. It stresses the joy and devotion of the individual, in addition to the study of Torah.

Havurah (ha-voo-RAH) is a group of Jews who pray and celebrate in members' homes, with or without a rabbi, and develop their own style of worship. Plural: **havurot** (ha-voo-ROT)

Hebrew (HEE-brew) is a Semitic language with a long history. It is the original language of the Bible, and was read and written by Jews wherever they lived. It is now the offical language of the state of Israel.

The Holocaust (HALL-uh-cost) was the persecution and mass destruction of European Jewry and other groups, such as the gypsies, by Nazi Germany from 1933 to 1945.

Humash (hoo-MOSH or HOO-mush) is a book containing the Torah, also called the Five Books of Moses, and the **haftarot**.

Judaism (JOO-duh-ism) is the religion and civilization of the Jewish people. The Jewish religion is based on the belief in one God and in a set of ethical precepts. As a civilization, it is made up of the common experiences, historical, cultural, and national, shared by the Jewish people.

Kiddush (kee-DOOSH or KID-dush) means "sanctification." It is the prayer recited over wine on the Sabbath and festivals. The word also refers to the reception after synagogue services at which the **Kiddush** prayer is said.

Kippah (kee-PAH) is a skullcap, a head covering worn as an ancient Jewish form of respect for God. **Yarmulke** is Yiddish for **kippah**. Plural: **kippot** (kee-POAT)

Kosher (Kah-SHER or KO-sher) is a term used for foods and eating utensils which means that they are ritually acceptable according to the Jewish dietary laws.

Maftir (mahf-TEER or MAHF-teer) is the name given to the concluding verses of the Sabbath or festival Torah reading. It is also the term for the person who is called to read these verses and who then chants the haftarah.

Matriarchs (MAY-tree-arks) refers to the foremothers of the Bible: Sarah, Rebekah, Rachel, and Leah.

Mehitzah (muh-HEE-tzuh) is the partition or screen in a synagogue that separates the women from the men.

Minyan (min-YAHN or MIN-yahn) is the quorum of ten adult Jews necessary for prayer services and other religious ceremonies. Traditionally only men were included in this quorum; today, excluding all Orthodox and some Conservative synagogues, women are counted too.

Mitzvah (mitz-VAH or MITZ-vah) is a religious commandment. Traditionally, there are 613 commandments, 248 positive and 365 negative. The word has also come to mean "good deed." Plural: **mitzvot** (mitz-VOTE)

Ner Tamid (ner tah-MEED or ner TOH-mid) means "eternal light" and refers to the lamp that hangs before the Holy Ark, the cabinet that holds the Torah scrolls.

Orthodox Judaism (OR-thuh-dox) is the movement that accepts both the Torah, the written law, and the Oral Law as God-given. The Oral Law is made up of those laws and commentaries handed down through thousands of years by the Rabbis. The Orthodox believe these laws and teachings may not be changed, but must be strictly observed.

Parashah (pa-ra-SHAH or PAR-shuh) is the weekly portion from the Torah that is chanted during the Sabbath service. Plural: **parshiyot** (par-shee-YOTE)

Rabbi (RAB-bye) comes from the term **rav**, which means "master," and originally signified a sage or scholar. Today the term refers to a Jewish religious leader. Plural: rabbis or **rabbanim** (rahb-bahn-EEM)

Reconstructionist Judaism (re-kun-STRUCK-shun-ist) is a movement founded by Rabbi Mordecai Kaplan in 1922. This movement stresses that Judaism is not only a religion, but a civilization, and constantly changing way of life.

Reform Judaism is a movement that arose in Germany in the early 1800s and advocated the continued evolution of Judaism in light of contemporary life and changing times.

Rosh Hodesh (rosh HO-desh) means "head of the month," and is the first day of the new Hebrew month. It always coincides with the new moon and is traditionally a semi-holiday for women.

Shabbat (Shah-BAHT), or **Shabbos** (SHAH-bus), the Sabbath, is the seventh day of the week, the day of rest and abstention from work, in honor of the day God rested from the work of creating the world. This weekly Jewish holiday begins at sundown on Friday night and lasts until one hour after sundown on Saturday.

Shaharit (SHA-ha-reet) is the morning service. It comes from the Hebrew word shahar meaning "morning."

Shema (shuh-MA) is one of the most important Jewish prayers; it begins by proclaiming the Oneness of God. The Shema and its special blessings form a central part of the daily prayers.

Siddur (see-DOOR or SID-der) is the Jewish prayer book.

Suffrage (SUF-fridge) is the right to vote.

Synagogue (SIN-uh-gog) is the Jewish house of prayer, study, and meeting.

Tallit (tal-LEET) or **tallis** (TALL-us) is a four-cornered prayer shawl with fringes at each corner. Plural: **tallitot** (tal-leet-OAT) or **tallesim** (tah-LACE-im)

Talmud (tahl-MOOD or TAHL-mood), part of the Oral Torah, means "study" or "learning." The term refers to the Aramaic text compiled during the first five centuries c.e.—a vast collection of Rabbinic law, thought, commentaries, and stories.

Tefillah (tuh-fee-LAH or tuh-FEE-luh) means prayer.

Tikkun (tee-KOON or TEE-koon) refers to a book that contains the Torah in both its printed and scribal form. The scribal half of the **tikkun** looks much like the words in the handwritten Torah scroll—without vowels or musical signs. People who are preparing to chant a Torah portion often study with a **tikkun**.

Tkhines (tuh-HEE-nuss) refers to a separate women's literature of personal prayers dealing with women's concerns, written in Yiddish, that developed in Eastern Europe.

Torah (Toe-RAH or TOE-ruh) refers specifically to the Five Books of Moses (Genesis, Exodus, Leviticus, Numbers, and Deuteronomy), whether written on a parchment scroll or in a printed text.

Trop (TROP) is a series of musical notations found in the printed text of the Bible either above or below each word. The melodies associated with the **trop** differ somewhat for the Torah reading and the haftarah.

Tzedakah (tzuh-dah-KAH or tzuh-DOK-uh) means "justice" or "righteousness." It is often translated as "charity." Jewish law recommends giving between 10 and 20 percent of one's income, plus gifts, to those in need.

Tzitzit (tzee-TZEET) or **tzitzis** (TZITZ-iss) is the fringe attached to each of the four corners of a **tallit** as a reminder of God's commandments. Plural: **tzitziyot** (tzee-tzee-YOTE)

Yiddish (YID-dish) is a language of medieval German origin which includes some words from the Hebrew, Romance, and Slavic languages. It was the daily language of most Eastern European Jews.

Zionism (ZI-uh-nism) is the movement whose goal is the return of the Jewish people to the land of Israel.

NOTES ON SOURCES

Much of the material for this book came from personal interviews: twenty-five in total. The rest of my source material were books and magazine and newspaper articles.

Some books that were especially helpful are *The Story of the Women's Movement* by Maureen Ash; *Jewish Women in Historical Perspective* edited by Judith R. Baskin; *The Jewish Woman in America* by Charlotte Baum, Paula Hyman, and Sonya Michel; *To Pray As a Jew* by Rabbi Hayim Halevy Donin; *Coming of Age: Your Bar/Bat Mitzvah* by Benjamin Efron and Alvan D. Rubin; *The Schocken Guide to Jewish Books*, chapter 11: "Jewish Women's Studies" by Rabbi Sue Levi Elwell; *Written Out of History: Our Jewish Foremothers* by Sondra Henry and Emily Taitz; *The Woman in Jewish Law and Tradition* by Michael Kaufman; *The Jewish Woman* edited by Elizabeth Koltun; *The Memoirs of Glueckel of Hameln* translated with notes by Marvin Lowenthal; *Bar Mitzvah, Bat Mitzvah* by Bert Metter; *Standing Again at Sinai: Judaism from a Feminist Perspective* by Judith Plaskow; *Putting God on the Guest List: How to Reclaim the Spiritual Meaning of Your Child's Bar or Bat Mitzvah* by Rabbi Jeffrey K. Salkin; and *Four Centuries of Jewish Women's Spirituality* edited and with introductions by Ellen M. Umansky and Dianne Ashton.

The magazines I used include *The Atlantic Monthly,* August 1993, for Cullen Murphy's "Women and the Bible"; *Keeping Posted*, January 1982, for information on Judith Kaplan Eisenstein's bat mitzvah ceremony; *Lilith: The Independent Jewish Women's Magazine,* Fall 1994, for Vivienne Kramer's article "Bat Mitzvah in the 90's"; *Reconstructionist,* April–

May 1989, for Rabbi Sandy Eisenberg Sasso's article "Growing Up: Expanding Our Bar and Bat Mitzvah Horizons"; *Reform Judaism*, Winter 1992, for Janet Marder's article on "When Bar/Bat Mitzvah Loses Meaning" and Danny Siegel's "Bar/Bat Mitzvah Heroes"; and *Sh'ma,* February 1991, for Joseph C. Kaplan's "Bat Mitzvah Celebrations."

The Jewish Women's Resource Center in New York City was a gold mine for finding newspaper articles about the bat mitzvah ceremony. Most of these articles came from *The Baltimore Jewish Times* (for the article about Alison Geare's shared bat mitzvah ceremony with Amy Joyce Glass) and New York's *The Jewish Week* (for articles about Shira Rockowitz and the Eldridge Street Synagogue, the Kofman twins, Alisa Jancu and the Altmans of Tashkent; and Yiling Livia Chen-Josephson's bat mitzvah ceremony in Kaifeng).

Speeches by Ayala Danya Galton and Sonia Rebecca Scherr came from Hanna Tiferet Siegel's personal collection of bar and bat mitzvah talks.

Finally, since it is not included in the text, here is the address for Mazon, A Jewish Response to Hunger: 2970 Westwood Blvd., Suite 7, Los Angeles, CA 90064.

INDEX

Abrabanel, Benvenida, 25, 27
Abraham (Patriarch), 10–11
Ackelsberg, Martha, 46–47, 120–21
Ackerman, Paula, 44
Aguilar, Grace, 38
Aharoni, Malia, 106
aliyah, 61, 62, 86
Anthony, Susan B., 7
anti-Semitism, 17, 22, 25–26, 29, 38
Ark, 84–86
Ashkenazi, Boula, 25
Avner, Sylvia, 73

Baal Shem Tov, 36
Bailey, Dena Landowne, 103–5
Bailey, Sheila Stein, 105
Bannett, Shoshana, 99–100, 110, 114, 116, 118, 119–20
bar mitzvah, 74; defined, 1–2
bat mitzvah: as an adult, 48, 60, 107, 119; afterward, 118–23; celebration of, 110–17; defined, 1–2, 74; description of ceremony, 47–48, 53–54, 83–96; history of, 5–9; how the different movements view, 51–58; importance of, 71, 78, 80–82, 97–100, 103, 105; preparation for, 51, 58, 60–82; unusual ceremonies, 106–9

Berger, Rabbi Kenneth R., 73
Bernstein, Carrie, 80, 100, 121–22
Bernstein, Laila, 80, 101
Bible: Five Books of Moses, 63, 64; stories from, 10–18; *see also* Torah
bimah, 6, 55, 56, 60, 61, 62, 71, 84–85, 92, 94, 100, 103
blessings, 61–62, 86, 91, 92, 94, 95, 102
booklet, 76–77, 102
Bruriah, 20

ceremonies, initiation, 78–80
chanting, 60–67
charity. *See tzedakah*
Chen-Josephson, Yiling Livia, 107–8
Christianity, 22, 24, 27, 28, 30, 45, 51
coming of age, 1–2, 78–79, 82
commandments (*mitzvot*), 9, 32, 62, 63, 74
community, 81–82, 85, 102, 111–12, 119–23
Conservative Judaism, 45, 46, 47, 51, 52, 53, 54, 55, 86, 87
converso, 25–26

David (king of Israel), 16–17
Deborah, 15–16

Deutsch, Elaina, 75–76, 99, 114,
  118
Diamond, Rachel, 60, 98–99,
  116, 117
dietary laws. *See* kosher
dowry, 23–24
Dvar Torah, 2, 53, 61, 70, 94,
  103, 105, 111; defined, 67–69

Egypt, 13, 23, 63, 91
Eilberg, Rabbi Amy (first
  woman ordained by the
  Conservative movement), 45
Elwell, Rabbi Sue Levi, 8, 123
equality, 7, 46, 55
Erdstein, Elana, 74–75
Esau, 11
Esther, 17, 28–29
Eve, 10, 72

Five Books of Moses. *See* Bible;
  Torah
Frank, Anne, 76
Franklin, Henrietta, 43

Galton, Ayala Danya, 68
Geare, Alison, 109, 133
genizah, 23
Gershom ben Judah, 24
ghettos, 22
Glueckel of Hameln, 33–34, 35
God, 62, 72, 77, 87, 89, 90, 92,
  94, 98, 100, 101
Goldin, Josee, 67, 68–69, 110,
  113, 117, 119
Goldman, Elizabeth, 102–3

Goldman, Emma, 43
Gottlieb, Rabbi Lynn, 45, 64,
  70–71, 78–80
Gratz, Rebecca, 37

Hadassah, 41
haftarah, 6, 53, 61, 62, 64–65,
  68–69, 72–73, 86, 94, 103;
  defined, 66–67
Hagar, 10
hallah, 73
Hannah, 16–17
Hasidism, 36
havdalah, 97
havurah, 46, 51, 53, 102
Hebrew, 31, 37, 61–62, 64, 65,
  86, 101–2, 107
Hebrew Union College-Jewish
  Institute of Religion, 8, 44–45
Hodel, 36
Holocaust, 71, 108, 121, 123
Horowitz, Sarah Rebecca
  Rachel Leah, 32
Humash, 64–66, 86
Husbands-Hankin, Shonna,
  57–58, 69, 113

industrialization, 35, 39
initiation, 78–80
Inquisition, 25–26
Isaac (Patriarch), 10–11, 32
Ishmael, 11
Islam (Muslim) and Islamic
  countries, 22–24, 27, 45
Israel, 27, 37, 69, 106–7, 121; *see
  also* Palestine

Jacob (Patriarch), 11–12
Jancu, Alisa, 108
Jerusalem, 57, 69, 84, 85, 106
Jewish woman: in Biblical times, 10–18; in Talmudic times, 19–21; in the Middle Ages, 22–29; in the 1500s and 1600s, 30–34; from the 1700s to modern times, 35–48
Jews: in Europe, 22–28, 30–40, 52, 111, 115, 121; in the United States, 37–48, 53–61, 64, 67–80, 97–105, 108–22; Sephardic, 25–26, 38, 73; under Muslim rule, 22–29
Judah ben Tema, 1
Judaism: changes within, 8, 36; modern branches of, 44–45, 51–53; see also Conservative; Orthodox; Reconstructionist; Reform

Kaddish, 96
Kanefsky, Rabbi Yosef, 54
Kaplan, Judith (Judith Kaplan Eisenstein), 5–6, 8, 48, 132
Kaplan, Rabbi Mordecai, 5–6, 7, 8, 45, 52
Kiddush, 95, 96, 103, 110, 115
Kiera, Esther, 28–29
kippah, 56, 57, 84
klezmer music, 115
Kofman, Stacey and Jana, 107
Kohut, Rebekeh Bettelheim, 40–41

Koller-Fox, Rabbi Cherie, 56–57
kosher (dietary laws), 41, 113
Krausen, Suzette, 98, 113, 121
Kushner, Rabbi Lawrence, 111–12

Lazarus, Emma, 38, 76
Leah (Matriarch), 12
Lemlich, Clara, 43
Levinthal, Helen Hadassah, 44
Licoricia of Winchester, 27–28
Lindheim, Irma Levy, 44
literacy, 30, 31, 37–38

maftir, 63–64, 92, 103
Maid of Ludomir. See Werbermacher, Hannah Rachel
Marrano, 25, 38
marriage, 23, 24
Married Women's Property Act, 7
Masada, 106
Matriarchs, 10–12, 32, 107
Mazon, A Jewish Response to Hunger, 112, 133
mehitzah, 53, 54, 103
menstruation, 78, 79
Meyer, Dr. Michael, 45
Michal, 16–17
mikvah, 9, 32
minyan, 8, 46, 54
Miriam, 13
mitzvah, 74–75; see also commandments
Montefiore, Lady Judith, 39

morning prayer service
(*shaharit*), 58, 90
Morpurgo, Rachel, 37
Morse, Ayana, 68, 97–98, 116,
117, 119
Moses, 13, 63, 71, 78; *see also*
Bible
Mott, Lucretia, 7
Muslim. *See* Islam and Islamic
countries

Namnah of Baghdad, 24
Nasi, Doña Gracia, 25–27
Nathan, Maud, 43
National Council of Jewish
Women, 40
ner tamid, 85
Neumark, Martha, 44

ordination of women, 44–45
Orthodox Judaism, 45, 48, 51,
52, 53–55, 69, 86, 87, 102–3,
105

Palestine, 39, 41
parashah, 63, 69–71
parents, non-Jewish, 55, 107
Perlmutter, Ariela, 99, 102, 115,
116, 117, 119
Polcelina, 27
prayer, 31, 54, 58, 76–77, 86, 87,
88, 90–91, 96, 101; *Shema,* 72,
90, 109
Priesand, Rabbi Sally (first
woman rabbi), 8, 45
prophets, 6, 15, 62, 64, 66

rabbi, 19–20, 52, 85, 91–92,
95–96; first woman, 8, 43–47;
Talmudic-Middle Ages,
23–24
Rachel (daughter of Kalba
Salvua), 20
Rachel (Matriarch), 12, 106
Rebekah (Matriarch), 11–12
Reconstructionist Judaism, 5,
45, 47, 51, 52, 53
Reform Judaism, 44, 47, 51, 52,
53, 55
refusenik, 108
responsibility, 1, 56, 60, 62, 74,
76, 82
Rockowitz, Shira, 115–16
Rodin, Alison, 100
Rosh Hodesh, 53, 63, 66, 97;
defined, 78; history of, 78–
79
Ruth, 16

Sabbath (Shabbat), 2, 6, 9, 32,
53, 55, 58, 62, 66, 73, 91, 94,
95, 97, 120; defined, 87–88
Sadker, Myra and David, 81
Salaman, Nina Davis, 39
Salkin, Rabbi Jeffrey, 112
Salome, Queen, 19–20
Samuel, 16
Sarah (Matriarch), 10–11, 32
Sarah Bat Tovim, 32
Sasso, Rabbi Sandy Eisenberg
(first woman ordained by the
Reconstructionist move-
ment), 45, 78

Saul (king of Israel), 16–17
Schapiro, Katya, 101–2, 113–15
Scherr, Sonia Rebecca, 72
Schneiderman, Rose, 43
scribe, 2, 65
scroll, 48, 63, 64, 66, 84, 92
Senesh, Hannah, 73
sermon. *See Dvar Torah*
shaharit. See morning prayer
   service
Siegel, Danny, 74
Siegel, Hanna Tiferet, 60, 68,
   71–72, 74, 78, 120
Silver, Cheri Ellowitz, 81–82
Solomon, Hannah Greenbaum,
   40–41
Stanton, Elizabeth Cady, 7
suffrage. *See* vote
Sullam, Sarra Coppio, 30–31
sultan, 25–29
Sweet, Sher, 60, 77
synagogue, 6, 35, 37, 53–55, 62,
   63, 100, 101, 121; description
   of, 83–87; Eldridge Street,
   115–16
Szold, Henrietta, 41

tallit, 36, 56, 57–58, 73, 78, 90,
   92, 98, 100; defined, 83–84
Talmud (Oral Law), 19–20, 52,
   105
tefillin, 36, 78
Temple, 46, 63, 74, 85, 107
tikkun, 65

Tiktiner, Rebecca, 32
tkhines, 31–32
Torah, 2, 6, 33–34, 48, 52, 53,
   61, 62, 63–67, 84–87, 91–92,
   95, 97, 98, 99, 103, 120; defined, 63; stories from, 10–15
trop, 64–65, 103
tutor, 58, 60–61, 66, 70–72, 74,
   92, 101
tzedakah, 75, 112
tzitziyot (fringes), 57

unions, 36, 43

vote (suffrage), 7–8, 34, 36, 43

Wald, Lillian, 39
Weissler, Chava, 32
Werbermacher, Hannah
   Rachel (Maid of Ludomir),
   36–37
Western Wall, 69, 107
women: female rabbis, 8,
   43–47; position of, 21, 23–25,
   27, 28–29, 34, 36, 47, 79–80;
   women's movement, 7, 40,
   43–44, 56

yad, 84
Yael, 15–16
Yiddish, 31, 32, 33, 76, 115

Zelophehad, 13–15
Zonderman, Shoshana, 102

Barbara Diamond Goldin is the author of *Just Enough Is Plenty*, winner of the National Jewish Book Award; *Cakes and Miracles*, winner of the Association of Jewish Libraries Award; and *The Passover Journey*, an ALA Notable Book (all Viking and Puffin). She lives in western Massachusetts.